Acclaim for IT'S A FREAKIN' MESS

Brilliant, entertaining and wise. For any of us smarting from the actions of divisive politicians or reeling from the onslaught of partisan opinions, Gillett offers a compelling different approach.

Dr. ELSPETH McADAM

Psychiatrist, co-originator of the *ability-spotting* treatment modality, author of *The Smoke that Thunders*

This book is invaluable for understanding *all* divisive times, and for transcending the divisive forces within our society. Gillett's step-by-step explanations and empowering exercises lead the reader beyond outrage to the freedom to exercise genuine agency in responding to our world. A skilled coach and guide, he's always on the reader's side, bringing compassion, insight, creativity, wit, *and* practicality to his commitment to helping us thrive.

JUDITH N. LEVI, PhD

Associate Professor Emerita in Linguistics at Northwestern University, recipient of the *Cross of the Order of Merit of the Federal Republic of Germany* in recognition of her "exceptional achievements in promoting reconciliation between the German and Jewish peoples"

I'm not much of a reader of books, but this one got me involved. Gillett deals with the most pressing issue in our so-called civilized society—*us versus them*. And refreshingly, he provides realistic solutions on how to be happy and effective when everything is a *Freakin' Mess* around us. Bravo.

KENNY WERNER

Author of *Effortless Mastery*

i

It's a Freakin' Mess: How to Thrive in Divisive Times is a short manual on how to retake the helm of our peace of mind and navigate the divisive waters of our time. I love this book. The greater the readership, the less divisiveness in the world! Truly a life-changing read.

LAURA ROGORA

Adult education consultant, Kansas City, former Professor of English, University of Buenos Aires

I have to admit that I want to hide my head in the sand at election time. Unsubscribe from it all. Shut off screens with activists and their certainty and the rising decibels in my ears. Gillett gives me a plan that is delightfully direct and doable. Hurrah! Now I can be with the people I tended to avoid. Thank you Dr. Gillett!

CAROL SANFORD

Senior Fellow in Social Innovation at Babson College, and multiple award-winning author of five best-selling books, including *The Regenerative Life*

Dr. Richard Gillett brings ancient wisdom and modern neuroscience right into our daily lives as we navigate today's climate of political and interpersonal divisiveness. *It's a Freakin' Mess* is an invaluable and user-friendly manual for how to live life with an open heart and discerning mind.

PATTI HOLLAND

Assistant Director for Mindfulness in Public Health and Medicine, The Mindfulness Center at Brown University

A brilliant prescription for transcending the crisis of disconnection in the world today.

ROBERT ALTER

Author of *The Transformative Power of Crisis*

It's a Freakin' Mess: How to Thrive in Divisive Times is a book about transformation – how we can change our inner turmoil about political and social issues into peace and equanimity even as we work to make this world a better place. Dr. Gillett shows how anger and fear shut down our higher brain centers and cause us pain, and, conversely, how we can remedy this by practicing open-heartedness. I tried this — through one of Dr. Gillett's short exercises — and found that it changed my state from fear of the people on the opposite side of an issue to a sense of calm, and helped make the outcome positive for all of us. I highly recommend this book!

MARJORIE WOOLLACOTT, PhD

Neuroscientist, Emeritus Professor of Human Physiology at the University of Oregon, author of the multiple award-winning book, *Infinite Awareness*

I was bowled over. Gillett builds up a thoroughly compelling case for an entirely different way of looking at, and acting in, the very divided world we inhabit… the book demonstrates how we can be healed, even when we are surrounded by divisive forces. Timely and superb.

JOHN MARTIN

Author of *About Memory*

Richard Gillett gives us clear and practical tools on how to handle polarized feelings and conversations. Grounded in modern research on positive psychology and contemplative neuroscience, Dr. Gillett shows us how we can be released from worry or hostility, even when we strongly disagree with another point of view. This is a fun and compelling read. Get this book and go have a conversation!

Dr. DAVID HADDAD, Ed. D.,

Psychologist, Associate Professor
at William James College

It's a Freakin' Mess gives the reader a clear pathway to both understanding and safely navigating the fear and anger that consume most of us in these divisive times. And Richard Gillett accomplishes this incredible task through fascinating research and a firm grasp of contemporary media culture. It's a gift.

LESTER STRONG

Former anchor at WHDH-TV and
Chief Executive, AARP Foundation
Experience Corps, Director of
The Peaceful Guardians Project

Dr. Richard Gillett skillfully integrates positive psychology, modern neuroscience, and ancient writings on contentment to create a route for us to re-find our peace of mind. Truly, a book for our times.

DAVID KATZ, PhD

Professor of Neurosciences and Psychiatry,
Case Western Reserve University
School of Medicine

It's a
FREAKIN'
MESS

Also by Dr. Richard Gillett

Overcoming Depression: A Practical Self-Help Guide to Prevention and Treatment

"Doctors, nurses and other health workers, as well as people with depression, should read this outstanding book, which has been written by a wise and well-read clinician."

— *British Journal of Psychiatry* review

Change Your Mind, Change Your World

"This is a first! [This book] shows the mechanisms through which our beliefs become translated into our circumstances — it is brilliant, challenging, and liberating."

— Joseph Chilton Pearce,
author of *The Crack in the Cosmic Egg*

It's a
FREAKIN' MESS

HOW TO ~~SURVIVE~~ *thrive!*

IN DIVISIVE TIMES

DR. RICHARD GILLETT

KINGSTON BRIDGE PRESS

Published by Kingston Bridge Press.
Cover design: Stéphane Dehais
ISBN: 979-8-63-815282-6

DISCLAIMER

Do not eat this book. It is not a toy. Keep away from herbivorous pets, such as goats.

    The author of this book is not your healthcare provider. Any exercises, recommendations, or explanations are not a substitute for consultation with, or treatment by, licensed healthcare practitioners or psychotherapeutic professionals. The author of this book is not liable for any damages arising out of, or in connection with, the use of this book. Since this book provides content related to emotional and physical health, your use of this book implies your acceptance of this disclaimer.

    Do not read this book while operating a motor vehicle or heavy equipment.

For Sanchi

CONTENTS

This book is about how to regain peace of mind during divisive times, even when we think we can do little to change a political or social situation.

I wrote this book before the COVID-19 pandemic, which is another kind of *Freakin' Mess* that is more immediately daunting. But even this huge world event has been massively affected by political divisiveness. In several countries, the initial denial of the seriousness of the epidemic — through putting political bias above factual evidence — has cost us crucial time, which has resulted in the unnecessary deaths of tens of thousands of people. Partisan certainty in society and politics diminishes our intelligence — as this book demonstrates — which results in decisions that cost lives. Therefore we need — even more urgently, I think — to know how to navigate the ongoing, radical political divides and social prejudices that surround us. How to do this is the subject matter of this book.

In these pages you will find ways to transcend the toxic worlds of political and social divisiveness — with their constant invitations into worry or outrage — and stand in your innate strength, experiencing the pleasure of living according to your own values.

Yes, it *is* a freakin' mess out there — but *we* don't

yes

need to be. And when we're not, we have a better chance of being effective in changing our society for the better.

My impetus for writing this book came early one morning. I had awoken at about two o'clock, my mind churning with all the inflammatory political news I'd heard on TV the evening before. Lying awake for hours, restless, worried, and exasperated, I came to a decision: I would research, and hopefully find, the steps I need to take, not just to get through, but to feel good and be more effective while living in these times of division.

It's a Freakin' Mess: How to Thrive in Divisive Times is the result of my research, honed by testing out every solution: first on myself, then on my (willing) friends — and ultimately fine-tuning these solutions by incorporating the feedback I received from my website readers. This book is also based on a lifelong personal and professional quest: what does it take for a person to lead the best possible life, even when circumstances are rough?

According to a recent issue of *U.S. News & World Report*, more than 80 percent of Americans believe that their country is divided along racial, ethnic and political lines. The U.K. and many other countries are undergoing similar levels of divisive acrimony. These divisions create suffering for many people — and raise some questions of deep concern:

- How can we best handle our frustration with people in power who, we believe, are not telling the truth or are exaggerating for their own benefit, personal or political?

- How do we mend broken bridges between ourselves and friends or family after we've argued so heatedly — or distanced ourselves so coldly — over different political affiliations?

- How do we best handle our concern — or outrage — about the prejudices and unequal opportunities in our country?

- What can we do to help make our country less divided?

- How can we feel more at peace in ourselves, in the midst of so much distrust and anger?

These are some of the questions this book answers with actionable recommendations.

I trust that once you read *It's a Freakin' Mess* — and experience this book's liberating exercises — that you, too, will be able to feel peace within yourself; that you will find you can protect your heart from the anger-provoking influences of the media and party politics (while still participating as you choose); that you will be able to reconnect, if you so wish, with family, friends, or neighbors in spite of political or other rifts; and that, for you enjoyable and uplifting feelings will take the place of frustration or fear.

Ambitious? Yes.

Doable? Yes.

I believe you can feel free, happy, and at peace during divisive times. And that when this is so, you will be more effective at making the changes you want.

CHAPTER 1

Transcend Divisiveness

We human beings do not *have* to create divisions. We have an amazing capacity to relate to other people, whatever their apparent differences and beliefs. When we make heartfelt connections with others, we feel a sense of oneness with them, and we experience compassion, warmth, and respect. These are very pleasurable feelings. Experiencing ourselves as being one with others feels good, and this works with both those we know and those we have never met before.

But if this is true, how then can we make sense of the divisiveness that seems so pervasive, not just in this country but in so many societies in this world? Scroll through today's news and chances are you'll be looking at the latest roll call of suffering and injustice: political feuds and corruption, religious violence, racial prejudice, an increasing divide between rich and poor, destruction of poorer people's environments, partisan imprisonments, and so on.

These social divisions are all deeply personal. When your values are ridiculed by those with different beliefs, it hurts. In the U.S., the idea of the American Dream is that everyone willing to work hard has an opportunity for success because there is a level playing field. But when you find this "level playing field" is actually not level at all, you become aware of the suffering—financial, professional, and, perhaps most of all, in your heart, which, like everyone's, craves respect, kindness, and equality.

Oneness with others feels good for all parties. Divisiveness does not feel good to either party, even to the perpetrator of division. Take the divisiveness that drives prejudice, for example—prejudice against women, different religions, races, or nationalities; prejudice against those who have less money. There is a common illusion that the apparent winners in these battles between peoples—those who, until now, have maintained the upper hand of power—will feel good. But while those wielding prejudice might feel united, this kind of unity-against-others, even if buttressed with a thousand justifications, does not create happiness. It creates an inner world governed by anger against those we are prejudiced against and by fear of those same people. Anger and fear do not feel good. People with prejudices are not at peace.

Well, you might ask, if oneness with others feels so good, and if divisiveness is so destructive and feels so bad, why would anyone choose divisiveness? This is a question that has puzzled me for a long time. In addition to my passionate interest in trying to understand more about human nature, I have had the good fortune to live on four different continents—Africa, Europe, Asia, and North America. Participating in different cultures, I've been able to see more of my own assumptions and prejudices. I've also experienced the beauty and creativity of human diversity, and, sometimes at the same time, the heavy self-righteousness of divisive prejudice, which creates so much misery. As a psychiatrist, I wanted to know the mechanisms and the motivations for this extraordinary process of divisiveness that seems to be so disadvantageous to the human race. Surely, I thought, there must be cogent reasons for why we do this, and maybe if we could understand these reasons, there would be a way to make a change.

Why It's So Easy to Get Caught in Divisiveness

The commonest answer given to this question of why we choose the self-destructive path of divisiveness is that we human beings are hard-wired to be tribal and separate. Faced with horrific examples of what humans do to each other and reminded of these every day by the regular pounding of the news, it's easy to feel daunted or to shrug a sorry conclusion that humanity is irredeemably selfish and destructive by nature. I have found, however, that the reality is far more hopeful—that human divisiveness is not some inevitable, hard-wired, biological imperative that we can only do our best to find a way around. There is a good deal of evidence, which I will come to, that we are not hard-wired to be jerks. Yes, we inherit the important ability to fight when necessary and to defend ourselves and our families from others. Yet we also—and equally—inherit a capacity for profound empathy, and we are blessed with the amazing complexity of our cerebral cortex, which offers us a vast choice in understanding and reaction.

Still, there are many social forces that encourage divisive behavior. The media often sell copy and set their clickbait traps by fomenting outrage and other emotions. The more adrenaline an article can force you to secrete, the more likely you are to read on, the more likely you are to respond to advertisements, and the more likely you are to remember the article and post it. Divisions and anger make money for media moguls. Anger doesn't feel so great, it's true, but it is memorable, and the adrenaline can be quite addictive.

Politicians use divisive tactics to gain votes and cement power. Some politicians can be diabolically clever at homing in on a population's anger/dissatisfaction and redirecting it in blame of a minority group that has limited voting power. Hitler was brilliant at this. It is not easy for most of us to avoid an angry reaction to this kind of manipulative political behavior. Yet, damn it, if we *do* get angry, we've just been sucked into exactly what the divisive politician wants: anger on one side increases anger on the other in a truly vicious cycle. Anger versus counter-anger cements opposing positions and buttresses the divisive worldview.

Later in this book, I mention some ways around this trap. This is not just a political trap; it affects everyone because we each suffer from our own emotional reactions to what those in power do. Resentment, indignation, contempt, outrage, unease, worry, fear, and anger don't usually feel good to us—especially when we experience them over a long time.

Otherizing

There is another way of looking at divisiveness that I've found really helpful—it is the temptation to *otherize*. To *otherize* someone is to make the mental decision that this person is either an enemy or of no importance. The modern word *otherize* has not yet made the printed dictionaries, but it's already in all the online dictionaries. *Otherizing* is the devastating ability we have to view different human beings as *other*, or as nothings who are not worthy of human compassion and care. To *otherize* is to deny that the humanity in *me* is also in *you* or that the humanity in *us* is also in *them*. Mentally, we are turning others into lower beings—either temporarily or more permanently—without the normal human attributes of intelligence, kindness, and soul.

Otherizing is more obvious when we think of gangs, religious extremists, and violent racists who demonize those who are different, seeing them as abhorrent beings worthy of disdain or death. But otherizing comes in many forms that are not necessarily so extreme. Recently a man shared this with me:

> I have these neighbors, and I'd always had a nice cordial relationship with them. They were friendly, and so was I. Then, a while ago, I saw the sign of the politician they were supporting on the edge of their lawn in good view of our road. I was shocked. My whole feeling toward them pretty well instantly changed. I found myself indignant and, I have to admit, angry. I told my wife about the sign.
>
> "How could they support that guy?" I said to her. "Can't they see who he is? What's wrong with them? They must be crazy. So damn stupid!"

Now, my wife and I were *both* upset.

If I'm honest—and I'm not proud of this—I had contempt for these people. It was a horrible feeling to have. There was no pleasure in this feeling.

And, then, every time I saw their sign—which was every day—I felt bad. I even started to worry that drivers in the cars passing by might think that I shared the same political view as my neighbors.

I don't know quite how to change all this for the better.

Name-calling, judgments, and insults (like *crazy* or *stupid*) are telltale symptoms of otherization. It's useful to see this because then we can do something about it. When we otherize, suddenly all the others' humanity disappears and they become nothing but objects of derision. In this state there is no room for curiosity (*I wonder what his reasons were for voting the way he did*) nor for compassion. In most cases, as soon as we otherize, we suffer, since the otherizing emotions—like irritation, frustration, exasperation, mistrust, alarm, foreboding, fear, and anger—are unpleasant to experience.

But sometimes when we otherize, we do not feel anger, do not appear to suffer, and may be unaware of any issue at all. This happens when those we otherize are not experienced as enemies but as people of so little importance they are not noticed or taken seriously.

In May 2016, there was a public outcry in the United States when the pharmaceutical company Mylan raised the price of its epinephrine auto-injector, called EpiPen. Since the year 2009, Mylan had raised the price some 500 percent, to more than $600, for a standard pack of two EpiPens. The cost of the actual drug, epinephrine, is about $1. Epinephrine is another name for adrenaline, which has been around for a few million years in every human being who has ever lived. Extra adrenaline can be useful in moments of very severe allergy, and those who are in danger of going into anaphylactic shock can be saved from death by epinephrine auto-injectors.

Since EpiPen had virtually no competition in the U.S. and since people are willing to pay quite a lot to avoid dying, Mylan could get away with massive price increases. This was called *price-gouging* in the press and the company was accused of greed. But the press did not, so far as I know, look into the fact that such greed cannot manifest without *otherizing*.

When CEO Heather Bresch was asked about the 500 percent price increase, her reported reply was "this is business." Bresch, as the top executive of Mylan, paid herself over $18 million a year, which is also business. Other people scratch their heads and ask, how can a business person be so oblivious to human needs and potential suffering? The answer is simple and, I think, important. Otherization creates safe compartments that are watertight to compassion. If the CEO of Mylan worried that one of her own children might die if she would take a certain action, she would almost certainly avoid that action. But when, because of the 500 percent increase in the price of EpiPen, some children were more likely to die because their parents were uninsured and could not afford the $600 cost of a $1 drug, Bresch did not take any action to protect these children.

We can understand this difference because we can understand that compassion is often reserved for family and friends and those we frequently see, and it often does not extend to others, especially to those we will never meet. And this is just the point: otherization is the denial/cutting-off/avoidance of care for those we do not consider in our clan; the avoidance of compassion for, in short, the other. Those we do not see and those we consider outside our group are often denied by us the benefit of being seen as fully human, with feelings and soul. They are not fully recognized as families with playing-laughing-crying children and caring-worrying-loving mothers. The *mother*, symbol of compassion, loses her "*m*" and becomes *other*.

The example of EpiPen is one of hundreds you

and I could come up with. Otherization appears everywhere because it is a universal—though not inevitable—human possibility. In looking at otherizers, it is very, very easy to act as they do—to otherize *them.* Once we call any of these otherizers *greedy, selfish, stupid, evil, bigoted*—and a hundred other scathing adjectives we might come up with—we have otherized them. Oh, how easy it is to otherize.

Sometimes I otherize my wife. We are in the middle of an argument about some detail that is probably not highly important in the whole scheme of the infinite universe, and I find myself—if I pause to reflect—so determined to win my point that I have converted this person whom I love into an alien being who, in that moment, is not deserving of compassion, heart, or even just being listened to. Fortunately, this is temporary. When I regain my senses, I wonder with amazement why trying to win some trivial point seemed so vital at the time and how quickly that moment of otherization destroyed compassion. I can also look, with some pleasure, at how recognizing these moments of otherization gives me a different choice, even in the middle of a disagreement.

Designating an Enemy

Otherization of a perceived enemy, whether personal or political, costs us our contentment. When you are faced with a blatant and unrepentant political other-izer, I admit it is not so easy to avoid otherizing back. Yet, when you otherize a person, group, or society, you make an enemy that jumps around within your head. This creates a problem for your peace of mind. It's not easy to feel peaceful when there's an internal war going on.

The mental designation of *enemy* leads you to a natural emotional reaction of upset, fear, or anger. At this point, the enemy begins to jump around in your body as well as your mind—your body feels the physi-ology of your action hormones, that adrenaline-surged desire to fight or defend, fueled with the emotions of anger or fear. And, conversely, as soon as the adren-aline surges within the body, the mental designation of *enemy* is stamped with emotional power: *it must be true, I can feel it.* This play between emotion and judg-mental designation can be a vicious cycle of increasing aversion and agitation. None of this feels good. While the aversion is generically categorized in terms of the animal reactions of anger or fear, each of these prime emotions has many variants in us human beings. At the top of the next page are a few common variants of the emotions of anger and fear.

While short-term anger and fear may be useful in some immediate situations—and short-lived anger may sometimes feel good—long-term anger and fear (and

FEELINGS RELATED TO DIVISION	
Anger Related	Fear Related
Irritation	Worry
Indignation	Unease
Dislike	Restlessness
Contempt	Mistrust
Frustration	Alarm
Exasperation	Foreboding
Outrage	Dread

their many variants) are usually unpleasant to experience. In addition, there is a lot of evidence that anger, held over the long term, is correlated with more cardiac problems and other diseases, and a significantly higher chance of early death. More on this later.

There is an alternative. We can protect ourselves from the constant invitations to anger and fear, and we can thrive in the pleasure of elevated emotions. The art is to protect ourselves without closing our hearts. When we do not cast the other as an enemy within our own minds, there is no need for a fight/flight reaction of anger or fear (or any of their variants). And when we are not suffused with aversive emotion, we are more likely to be effective socially. The sense of open-heartedness that transcends division is peace-making internally—as well as externally—and deeply gratifying. In the state of openheartedness, there are a number of common elevated feelings:

FEELINGS RELATED TO ONENESS	
Contentment	Empathy
Calmness	Compassion
Inspiration	Care
Gratitude	Love
Wonder	Humility
Joy	Kindness
Awe	Curiosity

If you were to ask people which list of feelings they would prefer to experience, most would probably prefer the second list. Yet so many of us spend more time than we would like in the first list. This book is on the art of how to get from the first list to the second. How to convert, for example, *anger against* into *action for*. Since all feelings are contagious, the more we live in the second list, the more we help others to do the same.

There is an important caveat. Getting to the second list does not involve pretense. It doesn't mean bottling feelings with the tension of suppression, nor disappearing into some never-never land where action is avoided. On the contrary, we can be fully responsive and do everything we can to make a difference. When we do this using the elevated feelings that are available to us, we are far more likely to be successful, in addition to being happier—as you will see.

CHAPTER 2

Emotion, Money, and Votes

Politicians and the media relentlessly bombard us with invitations into emotion—excitement, foreboding, fear, tension, arousal, anger, alarm, longing, curiosity. It is primarily emotion that prompts us to click on advertisements, emotion that drives us to vote one way or another.

Divisive emotions, like anger and fear, can be particularly effective in getting people to buy and to vote. It's not always so easy to see this. Most of us are so accustomed to living in an atmosphere of worry and aggravation that it appears... well, *normal,* just the way things are in the modern world. We may not notice when our feelings are exploited for political or commercial ends, and it may be difficult for us to see the cost in terms of our everyday peace of mind.

Politicians

Most politicians use divisive tactics at least some of the time to gain votes and cement power. We all know this, but we may not fully realize the extent of the negative effect this can have on us, personally.

When a politician otherizes his opponents by calling them divisive names that imply *bad, selfish, stupid, greedy, inhuman* or *evil*, this tactic coheres the politician's base through the common emotion of anger or its many aversive expressions, such as indignation, dislike, frustration, contempt, outrage, or hate.

Otherization, as anyone who follows politics could observe, can be an enormously effective means of building one's power base. It has been used for millennia to generate support for the ascendency of one tribe, one political party, or one nation over another.

The most famous example from last century was the ability of Adolf Hitler to generate intense otherization by the German people against Jews, Slavs, and anyone who was not Aryan—a category of human beings entirely invented by Hitler. This was a vivid demonstration of the destructive effect of otherization, the power of a single leader to disseminate it, and the viral nature of its spread.

The fear and anger generated by otherization cements populations into a stance of protection of the gang of *us* and aggression toward the gang of *them*.

These attacks can be scathingly obvious (as in, *they're nothing but cockroaches*) or they may be relatively subtle (as in, [name of politician] *denies her involvement in* [something horrible].) Either way, the attacks themselves inject us with the fire of adrenaline, using a poisoned dart that is often hard to trace.

When we think of the *us* as right and good, and the *them* as wrong and bad, our minds have been highjacked. The brilliant, multi-faceted mind turns into a simple switch that has only two modes of movement — *on/off, us/them, right/wrong.* Our capacity for complex thought has been reduced to black-and-white thinking. We can no longer see the shades of gray because our thoughts have become governed by the simpler needs of the emotional body. As soon as we are angry or fearful, these powerful emotions of self-preservation tend to direct the mind into one of two divisive priorities: protection of ourselves from the perceived enemy and attack against that enemy. The intellect then follows the emotional directive and comes up with any number of reasons to justify the division.

Political parties in general tend to encourage *we're-good/they're-bad,* black-and-white thinking. Such thoughts foster outrage, which stamps the black-and-white beliefs with even greater certainty — *I know I'm right! Feelings don't lie!* Political leaders regularly use this vicious cycle to hook supporters.

Gaining power over one group through demonizing another is effective because of—and this may sound strange—our natural capacity for empathy. On the most basic level, we empathize with others by resonating with their feelings. In this way, emotions spread, whether they are divisive or inclusive. Many politicians learn to use this human capacity for emotional connectedness in a divisive way. That is, they unify one group by attacking a second group.

Once a group has been united in anger, so long as the anger remains, each member becomes effectively less intelligent, less discerning, less able to see beyond blame. On a mental level, this is because anger directs the mind into ruts of *us/them* thinking—ruts that can sometimes be so deeply gouged that we cannot see over the edges to other possibilities. On a physical level, when we are angry, neuronal impulses are actually shut down in our forebrains (the prefrontal cortex, seat of rational thought), leaving our instant-action, lower brain dominant.

The shutting down of the forebrain during fear or anger is well-documented. What is scary is that this is not necessarily temporary. When fear and anger become habitual, they actually alter the structure of the brain! This is because brain tissue—like muscle tissue—grows with use and shrinks with disuse. Incessant dwelling in fear or anger causes shrinkage of the dendrites—the connections between neurons—in the prefrontal cortex, the primary seat of intelligent understanding. This physical shrinkage in the prefrontal cortex is combined with expansion of the dendrites in the primal amygdala, a key center in the fight and flight mechanism.

Politicians may not know the neurology of how anger diminishes intelligent discernment, but many know instinctively that if they can generate the passion of anger, they will have followers.

And some politicians are immensely clever at tapping into a population's anger or dissatisfaction over diminishing wealth, and redirecting this anger in blame of a minority group that has limited voting power. Another common tactic is to ramp up the rhetoric against another country, implying that the home country is in imminent danger of attack from this foreign power. Such tactics have been used for thousands of years to incite warlike coherence against a trumped-up enemy.

It is no easy matter to deal with a talented anger-generator. On the one hand, a politician's anger and insults may unite his base; we are highly social beings and emotions are extremely contagious. On the other hand, those who disagree may easily get caught in the same anger. The anger is directed in the opposite direction, that's true, but the anger is still the same emotion, with all the negative effects it has on us.

Either way, we've just gotten sucked into what the divisive politician has orchestrated: anger on one side increases anger on the other in an almost endless vicious cycle. Anger versus counter-anger cements the lines of battle and reinforces a divisive worldview.

This is not just a political trap. What those in power do affects us personally, because we suffer from our own emotional reactions—resentment, indignation, contempt, outrage, unease, worry, fear, anger. But if we recognize how these feelings may have been manipulated by party machines, that gives us a little more control. More on what to do about this in chapter 6.

Media

Listening to too much news is bad for your health. Physically and mentally.

On the mental level, our minds become disrupted by the frequent descriptions of conflict, the endless battles of party politics, the spats, the snubs, the spikes of sarcasm. The riling of our mind ruffles our emotions of fear, anger, or rage. These emotions inevitably affect our bodies. They increase muscle tension, reduce the quality of our sleep, and diminish our resistance to disease.

Many people take a news-media dose of hostility three or more times a day without ever thinking of the long-term effects. A daily diet of hostility is immensely bad for us. When we practice hostility, we develop the habit of hostility. Over time, our habits become our personality. And beyond this, several medical studies have shown a statistical correlation between the chronic harboring of hostile thoughts and death through disease.

In one such study published in the journal *Psychosomatic Medicine*, 255 physicians were psychologically rated for personality traits, including a rating for hostility (Ho score). A follow up was done with these medical doctors twenty-five years later. Doctors who'd had a Ho score in the upper half of the Ho range at the age of twenty-five were more than four times more likely to have developed coronary artery disease by the time they were fifty than were their colleagues with lower Ho rankings. The doctors with higher Ho scores were nearly seven times more likely to die from any cause. In another retrospective study on 118 law students, 20 percent of students who were in the top quarter of Ho scores were dead before they reached fifty, as compared to 4 percent of students in the lowest quarter of Ho scores.

How much the news media contribute to the morbidity and mortality from hostility is of course impossible to measure. There is also a lot of variation between news sources in how much they ignite partisan hostility. Nearly all news media, however, are more or less dependent on some drama and outrage for their sales.

While drama can be positive or negative, more of it is negative. The media gains readers or viewers by inciting various emotions, such as anger, fear, surprise, suspense, curiosity, inspiration, excitement. Some media use clickbait traps to incite these same emotions. Clickbait works even when we know we're being played with, when we can clearly see the angler's hook and line clumsily knotted to the bait.

Clickbait is not necessarily negative — some clickbait can lead us to useful information. *Outrage clickbait* — whether informative or not — is designed to fire our adrenaline response. This can be in the smallest of ways. Here's one that invaded the phones of millions of people who might, just once, have shown some interest in the quirks of British royalty: "Kate snubs Meghan Markle?"

The question mark might appeal to your sense of curiosity — *Well, did she or didn't she?* — while the snub invites you into some small amount of mildly entertaining outrage.

Click. You read the article, navigating your little boat of intention past the countless rocks of ads as best you can without inadvertently hitting one, until you finally find out that, no, Kate did not snub Meghan Markle—not even a tiny bit.

Now you're no longer upset at Kate; you are upset at having been hooked by the clickbait (even though you saw the hook) and having just wasted another ten minutes of your precious time. And yet, evidence shows, we fall for these kinds of baits over and over again, even after repeated disappointments.

The more adrenaline an article can force you to secrete, the more likely you are to read on, the more likely you are to remember the article and post it, and the more likely that you (and the others you posted it to) will respond to the advertisements. The more adrenaline a show can make you secrete, the more likely you are to watch it and to recommend it to others, thereby contributing to audience numbers and advertising revenue.

When the adrenaline-raising techniques are used on political issues that are already inflammatory, it is easy to hook an audience into angrifying divisions. Some media are unashamedly partisan and deliberately foster hostility against the other side. They choose presenters or hosts who are skilled at riling emotions against the enemy.

Some of these hosts are overtly angry: their hostility is contagious and often spiked with ridicule.

Other hosts use more satire and sarcasm: they get their audiences laughing at the enemy.

All of this has entertainment value. There is excitement in getting mad at *them*, or in laughing at *them*. I don't mean to put down laughter, which, of course, can be fun, releasing, therapeutic—it's just that when our laughter contains derision, there is an edge of anger that riles both us and them.

Partisan performances by TV hosts, otherizing news articles, and angry politicians create alarm in our mental and physical systems. Repeated alarm creates the toxicity of accumulating adrenaline responses, and we, the news imbibers, end up living in a more or less perpetual, internal, toxic environment.

But we can quite easily protect ourselves from the divisive influences of media and of politicians—the subjects of chapters 5 and 6.

CHAPTER 3

How Divisive Emotions Can Save or Ruin Your Life

For most of us, divisiveness doesn't feel good at all. Why, then, do we get caught so easily in divisive emotions like indignation, exasperation, contempt, outrage (and other varieties of anger)? Or mistrust, worry, foreboding, alarm (and other varieties of fear)? And why are these feelings sometimes so hard to get out of? Yes, it's true that forces in society can tempt us into angry or fearful feelings—but what is it in us that responds? And when are anger and fear useful to us, and when are they not?

When I was ten, I witnessed a scene I have never forgotten. I was living in Uganda, where my father was employed as researcher on mosquito-borne disease. Family friends had driven my sister and me to see a local pride of wild lions. We found the lions, lazing in the warm African sunshine on an open patch of dry earth interspersed with tufts of grass. There was another vehicle there, a van with six people inside. A large male lion with a magnificent mane was lying in the foreground. Perhaps he was protecting the pride's private siesta from the strange metal-packaged intruders, but if so, he looked surprisingly relaxed — his eyes were three-quarters closed and his head rested on his paws. It was quite a picture. Little did I know that this idyllic scene was about to change dramatically.

The driver of the van, for reasons only he could know, opened his door, which was facing the lions and about fifteen feet away from that magnificent male.

The reaction of the male lion was instant. From his recumbent posture, this four-hundred-pound, muscle-ripped creature-of-the-wild — armed with lethal teeth and eighteen daggered claws — sprang twelve feet into the air with electrifying speed and a blood-curdling roar.

I was open-mouthed in awe. I watched the dust of the African ground swirl in the air with the motion of the lion's leap. He landed on his four feet before the man in the van managed to close his vehicle's door. Had the lion decided to leap forward in attack, rather than straight up in the air, there is no doubt he could have reached and killed the man before the man could have closed the van door.

The van driver might have regretted his action, but I certainly didn't. I had been witness to a marvel of nature, the primordial might of raw animal power.

Anger and Fear as the Great Protectors

When I thought about this story years later, and remembered that this lion had leapt up vertically, it occurred to me that he could have made two other significant choices. The lion could have leapt backward in fear and flight, or he could have leapt forward with aggression and fight, attacking the man in the van. Perhaps the lion's vertical leap was somewhere between those twin pillars of biological alarm: anger/fear, fight/flight. Either way, it was a dramatic and effective display of force.

Anger and fear have identical physiological pathways: they are two sides of the one coin—aversion. Corner a wild rat and it will quiver with fear yet lunge with feral anger. Lions and human beings are much the same in that aversion can be expressed either in anger and attack, or in fear and retreat.

When we are in physical danger, our vital instincts for fight/flight are immensely useful. If a woman is about to be attacked by a lion, for example, nerve impulses will instantaneously instruct her adrenal glands to secrete a surge of adrenaline, cortisone, and other hormones. These hormones, and corresponding fight/flight nerve impulses, can have amazingly beneficial effects in such emergency situations.

- The emergency hormones increase the speed of breathing and dilate the bronchioles so that oxygen can reach the lungs and be transferred to the bloodstream with maximum efficiency.

- They increase the speed of the heart and dilate the blood vessels that supply the muscles, so that oxygen can be transferred via these blood vessels to the muscles, again with maximum efficiency.

- These first two functions increase the efficiency of the muscles so that the woman can run away faster or fight with more power.

- The hormones increase the emotions of fear and anger by energizing the more primitive parts of the brain. These primary emotions add passion and energy to the fight/flight response.

- At the same time the prefrontal cortex—the seat of rational thought—is switched off. Why? Because pondering the pros and cons of possible options is not so useful when you are being charged by a lion.

- The hormones increase the speed of blood clotting from potential wounds.

- At the same time, the hormones block functions that would take up energy and are not, in the moment, absolutely necessary for survival. For example, they shut down the immune system —fighting a charging lion takes precedence over fighting a cold.

- The surge of hormonal release also reduces the blood supply to the guts and the flow of digestive juices — hence the dry mouth and that queasy feeling that sometimes accompany a moment of fear. In essence, the body makes an instant and wise prioritization: digestion is not so important when running from a lion — the priority is to avoid being digested.

All of these effects, including the emotions of anger or fear, are beautifully geared for a short-term, physical emergency in times of danger. Fear can protect you from going too near to the edge of a cliff or from driving too fast around a hairpin turn. Anger can lend you incredible strength and speed when you need to fight or escape from immediate physical danger. Anger can also be a useful signal that informs those attacking you that they had better back off.

Anger and Fear as Liabilities
But in many situations that do *not* require physical

action, the emergency reactions of anger and fear are not helpful. And here's the problem: we still produce the same emergency anger/fear response even when we just *imagine* danger. If you take your pulse, then vividly imagine a really scary scene in which you're in danger, and then take your pulse again, you will probably find that your pulse rate has significantly increased. Your blood pressure, too, will have gone up. This is the adrenaline response without the lion.

Our bodies do not differentiate between a real attack on our physical being and an imagined attack. When we otherize any person or group, we are creating an imagined enemy to whom we respond with adrenaline-fired anger/fear. Since there is, in most cases, no physical danger, there is no physical activity we can do to lessen the danger we have created in our minds. What's more, the imagined danger tends to be long-term, and this can cause us a lot of grief.

When we think someone with different beliefs is the enemy and react emotionally to this "enemy" we have created, all the physiological effects of the adrenaline response, so useful in a physical emergency, become dangerous long-term liabilities.

- Because the body is functioning on an emergency system, it becomes depleted, then exhausted when the "emergency" state carries on for hours, days, months, or even years.

- Our access to rational thought diminishes because neuronal activity has been shifted from the thinking cerebral cortex to the instant-reaction primitive brain to prepare for the physical emergency that never arises. In the long term, this can cause loss of brain matter in the pre-frontal cortex.

- Digestion is poor because blood has been diverted to the muscles for action that never occurs.

- The immune system is compromised because it is not a priority for the physical encounter that never happens.

- Blood clotting increases to protect the body from the potential wounds in the physical battle that never transpires.

It is possible that this blocking of the immune system and increase in blood-clotting contributes to the higher death rate of more hostile people. We can make ourselves ill, even kill ourselves slowly, by engaging our innate physical protective devices in the long-term service of our mental beliefs. This is all the more alarming when you consider that most human hostility is created to fight alternative beliefs — not lions.

We also suffer mentally. If a challenge to one of our beliefs is experienced as a threat to us, we will do almost anything to get away from or destroy the perceived threat, and this is accompanied by an out-pouring of unpleasant-to-experience emotion—such as fear, anger, disgust, disdain, hatred, and so on.

Hard-Wired to be Fearful or Angry?

Our reactions of worry or exasperation arrive so quickly that they appear automatic. It's as if we had no choice. We might well wonder, *Am I just hard-wired to be like this?*

The fact that our bodies don't seem to know the difference between real danger and imagined danger *is* probably hard-wired. If this is so, our ingrained biological hardwiring for fight or flight might, at first sight, appear to be an insurmountable human weakness, a biological liability that too easily tempts us into being trigger-happy, irascible, and irresponsible idiots. But this would be true only if we overlooked one crucial point: *a biological tendency is not a biological imperative.*

We are also, and I think equally, hard-wired with the capacity for great empathy, kindness, and compassion. In addition, each of us has inherited the awesome complexity of the cerebral cortex with its tens of billions of neurons—and this gives us unparalleled choices in response to any situation. The human brain is remarkably adaptable and teachable. Whatever we do several times will tend to become habitual, and we, as human beings, always have a choice in what we decide to do.

In particular, knowing the fact that our bodies do not differentiate well between real and imagined danger, we have the power to change what we imagine! When we re-imagine the old mental enemy as one of us, for example, this in itself can change the *anger/fear* emotional reaction.

I've said several times that the animal fight/flight, anger/fear response is natural, and often effective when the danger is physical. But even this is a matter of choice for us human beings. Thousands of martial arts practitioners have learned how to respond even to physical danger without anger or fear, and they've found that they are actually more effective at dealing with the danger without the adrenaline response. We are truly creatures of stupendous free choice.

CHAPTER 4

The Tyrannosaurus
in the Room

Why do people from different political parties hate each other? Why do people who believe in a religion that espouses compassion kill those who believe in a different religion that espouses compassion? These questions are often answered in terms of the strong human desire to belong, to feel part of a group identity. And yet some people who enjoy group identity are highly tolerant while others are willing to kill, or die, in their passion to condemn those with different beliefs or different appearances. Clearly there is another factor involved.

This factor is both obvious and hidden, simple yet multifaceted. We all have it, and it is really easy to sense in other people—just as you can easily smell someone else's breath, but if you've ever tried to smell your own breath, it's impossible. Your nose and brain have already acclimatized to whatever resides in your mouth and consider it to be the norm and therefore A-OK.

Divisiveness is associated with a simple, often overlooked, tyrannosaurus-in-the-room feature—the human ego. I'm using the word *ego* in its colloquial and original sense, as in *he's got a big ego*—the sense in which the majority of people use the word. Our ego is our pride in being different from others.

Our ego makes itself bigger—sometimes ginormous—by

- Feeding on differences and comparisons,
- Allying itself with those it considers similar, and
- Diminishing anyone it considers different.

The ego sees itself as special. If the ego were honest, it might say to itself: *I am right, good, superior, or, at the very least, special; you are wrong, bad, inferior, or not nearly as special as I am. Even if I'm not as skilled at something as you are, I'm still more special than you—my personal history is special; my character is special; my characteristics are special; my beliefs are special; my feelings are special; my successes are special; my failures are special. I'm different from you, and that difference makes me special.*

It is this special-ness of the ego that makes it

possible for 90 percent of us to think that we are better drivers than average. It is the ego, equally, that enables any one driver (whatever speed he drives) to believe that anybody driving slower than he drives is a moron, and that anybody driving faster is crazy.

But what about the importance of self-esteem? Isn't it vital for everyone to have self-esteem? Should we not think well of ourselves?

There is a crucial difference between self-esteem and ego. "Self-esteem is how we feel about ourselves," a teacher told her pupils, "while ego is how we compare ourselves to others."

You can be proud of yourself without putting anyone else down or thinking you are superior. You can acknowledge your own life-given gifts, your humanity, your moments of courage, your kindnesses, your hard work. This recognition of your own greatness is a wonderful thing. And in being open to recognize your own greatness, you can also be open to recognize the greatness in others.

Self-esteem has nothing to do with superiority or inferiority to others. It is those who lack self-esteem who get caught in measures of superiority and inferiority. This can be confusing, because those who think they are superior, or who act with superiority, usually do not realize that they are trying to compensate for their lack of basic self-esteem. Bullies lack self-esteem as much as those who admire bullies or worship celebrities.

It is also true that many of us are brought up hearing messages from family or society that we are *less than.* This is both unfortunate and untrue. No one is *less than.* No one is *more than.* The reason it may be difficult to believe this is that most of us have been enticed into a make-believe world in which there are imaginary clubs of superior and inferior people. Most of us have been taught that we are in one of these clubs or, sometimes, in both of them. Unfortunately, when we believe we are members of one of these two clubs, it often becomes our experienced reality.

But, if, in our own hearts, we do not believe in these differentiating clubs, then even if others treat us as inferior or superior, we will not be so affected — except perhaps in the compassion of knowing that they are caught in their own prisons of limitation.

With regard to specific tasks, some people may of course perform "better" than others — but this has nothing to do with the *value* of the person. Each one of us has innate strength, compassion, courage, kindness, diverse talents. Each human physical body — over which each of us has some jurisdiction — is a phenomenon of unimaginable complexity. Your body contains, for example, more electrons than there are grains of sand on this earth! There are around 500 trillion of these moving electrons in each of your cells, and there are around 37 trillion cells in your body. It's hard to grasp the size of a number like 37 trillion—if you tried to count this number as fast as you could, without stopping to eat or sleep, it would take you more than 4000 lifetimes. And yet, each one of your 37 trillion cells is a powerhouse of flexible creativity, more complex than a space shuttle! You are truly a miracle of creation. Self-esteem is the humble recognition of this fact. "Wow, I'm amazing," you might say, "though no more amazing than you or you."

It is when we forget the fact of our innate greatness that we try to bolster our image of ourselves through comparison, through measures of superiority and inferiority that otherize those we consider different. This is the ego, the mental organ of otherizing.

So why do we have this ego? And does it have any positive attributes?

The ego can be seen as an intricate part of the anger/fear, fight/flight, self-protection system. This system is focused on the individual *against* others. When there is physical danger, we protect the individual self, or the group, against attack.

If a lion is charging you, you consider only your own needs and not the hunger of the lion. This is natural and very useful to your continuing existence.

In situations of danger, you see yourself as *good*,

in the sense of worthy of survival, and the attacking force as *bad,* in the sense of a danger to your physical integrity. It's an opportune time, you might say, to be selfish, and not an especially practical time to engage in being considerate.

I/you, us/them concepts are valuable for self-protection when there is physical danger to ourselves, to our families, and to those who are dear to us. Sometimes, otherizing the source of physical danger can be life-saving.

The problem occurs when we turn others into enemies based on differences in beliefs or physical appearance. Prejudice against an attacking lion is not only natural and useful, it's also short-lived—because the attack is short-lived, whichever way it goes. Prejudice against those who are different creates a scenario of permanent embattlement. It's permanent to the extent that the differences we focus on, and feel superior or inferior about, tend to become ingrained in our minds.

Making Enemies

It is actually impossible to have long-term prejudice against another person or group without the ego's pride in difference. Here's a summary of how the ego is inextricably linked to prejudice and otherizing:

- The personal ego is the mental organ of otherization—*I'm better, you're worse; I'm more worthy than you;* or, *whether I'm better or worse than you, I'm more special than you are.*

- Personal egos gang up to form collective egos—*we're right, they're wrong; those who are similar to us are good, those who are different are bad.*

- All prejudice is based on a single irrational process—*those who are different from us are less worthy than we are, and therefore less worthy of compassion, kindness, inclusion, respect, or self-determination.*

- Ego and prejudice are inseparable twins: prejudice cannot exist without the ego's pride in one's difference—*I'm different, therefore I'm better, or more worthy, or more special.*

- Prejudice creates counter-prejudice, which bolsters the original prejudice in an escalating vicious cycle.

> First ego: *I hate you because you are different.*
>
> Second ego: *I hate you because you hate me.*
>
> First ego: *Well, if you hate me, I hate you even more…*

The Ego's Disguise

Recognizing our own ego as a prime cause of our prejudice against others—*oh, it's me, not them*—can be kind of embarrassing. For this reason, we each tend to hide our ego... and then it lurks in the background—the invisible tyrannosaurus in the room. Despite the fact that the ego's pride in differences creates the misery of divisiveness, not many people want to see it, talk about it, and, no, certainly not admit it.

Since the ego, by definition, sees itself as primarily good and in the right, the ego-driven mind has enormous difficulty admitting its desire for specialness. How can the system for self-righteousness (the ego) ever admit that its apparent superiority is based on something so petty as the need to feel that it's better than another? The contradiction is stark: the ego sees itself as good and right, but the ego's need to feel superior to another doesn't look good or right. The ego usually handles this otherwise glaring inconsistency by a simple and automatic maneuver: disguise. It resorts to self-deception in order to maintain its good opinion of itself.

"All cruel people," wrote Tennessee Williams, "describe themselves as paragons of frankness."

They probably believe it too, such is the ego's capacity for disguise, even from its own self. Almost any liability can be airbrushed into an apparent asset, for example:

LIABILITY	➡	AIRBRUSHED SELF-PERCEPTION
Prejudice	➡	I'm very honest; I tell it like it is.
Vindictiveness	➡	I believe in justice.
Exploitation	➡	I'm astute; I'm smart.
Misuse of power	➡	I'm strong; I'm a great tactician.

How Our Ego Creates Anger and Fear

When there is no division into *good/bad, us/them* —when there is no enemy—it is easy to hold our thoughts lightly as possibilities or hypotheses. When we are not emotionally identified with our beliefs, we have no adrenaline reaction if they are challenged. It is fine for others to have different opinions. And we can enjoy the traditions we love without putting down anyone else's tradition.

But as soon as we define our specialness by contrasting ourselves with those who are different—as soon as there is ego invested in our belief—something else happens. If I think that a belief or label *is* me, *is* who I am, then any challenge to this belief feels like a challenge to my very own self. An attack on a belief we are identified with feels as if our very existence is being threatened, and we will do almost anything to get away from or destroy the perceived threat, which is accompanied by an outpouring of aversive emotion: fear, anger, disgust, disdain, hatred, and so on. This becomes a vicious cycle of divisive energy:

Attachment + aversion

- The more we identify ourselves with a thought, belief, political party, nationality (i.e., we believe *this is who I am)*, the more we see others with different beliefs as a threat—an enemy—to the identity we think we are.

- The more we see others as enemies, the more we suffer from our own adrenaline response to the enemies we have created in our minds.

- The stronger our adrenaline response, the more certain we are that we are right. Anger and fear confirm our sense of the danger of the other—*it must be true; I can feel it.*

The social brain connects with others through recognizing commonality and shared humanity. When we are in the mode of openness, we experience others as similar to us and we can feel the elevated emotions of empathy, compassion, ease, peacefulness, and care.

But as soon as we attack—or are attacked—with *we're right/they're wrong* beliefs, fueled by the ego's pride in difference, we move into self-protection mode (or identity-protection mode). We are no longer able to experience those heart-opening, connected feelings because our primary objective is to survive the assault of the enemy—even if it is an enemy we have helped create in our own minds.

Threats that Endanger our Survival

Not all enemies are created entirely in the mind, of course. Civil rights activists have been shot or attacked by dogs. People who have tried to protect the trees of the Amazon, and the livelihood of their families who live there, have been murdered.

In case of physical attack, our self-protective fight/flight response is natural and may be protective against a real enemy in that moment. There are many situations in which self-protection takes priority.

Often, though, we have more choices than lions do. Martin Luther King refused to see white people (including the violent minority) as the enemy. Through the strength of his belief, and his courageous renouncing of physical fight or physical flight, his movement changed the scale of overt prejudice in the U.S.

This chapter is on a key factor in most conflicts. It is our pride in differences — the human ego — that either starts or escalates most human battles. Those who killed civil rights activists suffered from the ego's pride in difference: *I'm better than you because my skin is a different color from yours (or from the skin color of the people you support).* Those who kill the people who try to protect their trees are also suffering from the ego's pride in difference — they believe that the indigenous people are so inferior to them, that their lives are unimportant. These are just two examples of the devastating potential of pride in difference. This one belief of the ego—*we are superior*—is at the heart of nearly every war and atrocity. Fights between political parties, enmeshed in self-righteous anger, are fueled by that same belief, the certainty, *we are better than you.*

The relevance of all this to us personally is that understanding it gives us a means to change it. Admitting to ego usually reduces ego, and since prejudice cannot exist without ego, this starts a beneficial process for all parties. Melting walls of prejudice allows the possibility that other views can be better seen and respected. The recognition of the play of ego creates an opening for greater humility and tolerance, and this, in turn, reduces our own suffering from the ravages of our own long-term adrenaline responses. We are almost invariably happier without our pride in our differences.

CHAPTER 5

Protect Yourself from Divisive Influences in the Media

It's three o'clock in the morning, and I'm lying in bed, upset about what I saw on TV about a decision a politician made that I believe will cause many people to suffer. I cannot change this politician's decision—certainly not in the near future and probably never—so the question is how do I handle my own reaction in a way that doesn't cause *me* to suffer?

Ongoing suffering about such matters is neither necessary nor useful. I don't mean that harshly. I just mean that such reactions don't really help anyone and that there are ways to avoid these reactions. There are many levels of dealing with this, which I will come to later. One of the simplest and most easily effective—the subject of this chapter—is to control our own input of divisive news. This is something over

which each of us has complete power. It is our decision when to take in divisive news, in what form to
take it in, and how much to take in.

Yet most of us don't even think to protect ourselves. When we see and hear about divisive politics,
it's easy to discount the effect this will have on us: *well,
it's the same old stuff; I'm pretty used to it by now.*

Yes, most of us are used to it, it's true, but still it
affects our mental and emotional state. Even if we don't
feel annoyed or upset at the time, angry or fear-laden
thoughts may reverberate later and reduce the quality
of our sleep or diminish the pleasure of our day.

As I mentioned in chapter 2, news sells best
when it exaggerates — or creates — drama and alarm.
The more adrenaline a media company can get you
to secrete, the more financially successful they will
be. One of the ways for media to get the adrenaline
running is through publicizing political conflict in
the news, adding spice in the form of out-of-context
quotes, and focusing on the moments of greatest ver-
bal or physical violence.

It is valuable, I think, to maintain a healthy skep-
ticism by looking at the ways in which a media article,
tweet, video, or newsfeed may be geared by financial
incentive to rile us, divide us, adrenalize us. And then
to question:

- Do I want to be a pawn of media corporations, making them money while I hurt myself, physically and mentally, by drinking the toxicity of repeated alarm?

- Do I want to be a pawn of the rumor mongers on social media, boosting their reader traffic while I hurt myself physically and mentally by drinking the toxicity of repeated alarm?

If you do not, there are at least three things you can quite easily change: you can change the *timing* of the news you take in; you can reduce the *quantity* of the news you take in; you can change the *tone* of the media you take in.

Change the Timing of Taking in News

Whatever our minds are engaged with right before we go to bed is what we tend to carry with us into the night. Then, in the silence and the dark, somehow our feelings, especially of fear or anger, tend to become magnified.

Fear or anger creates adrenaline; adrenaline interferes with the rhythm of sleep.

You may watch the news and go to bed with no awareness of any upset—until you wake up early with an unpleasant scene from the news replaying in your mind. Or maybe you awaken at your usual time without feeling refreshed because the rhythm and depth of your sleep has been affected by the tension you carried into the bedroom the night before.

When you see violent images — still or video — the long-term effects are often much greater. Eyes are the predominant sense organ in human beings, with the most connections in our brains, and images have a much more powerful emotive effect than words alone.

I mentioned waking at 3:00 a.m., upset about a political decision that I had seen on TV. And, yes, I'd been watching this program just before going to bed.

The logical answer? *Don't listen to the news before going to bed!*

"Hey, but wait," I tell myself, "I need to know what the news is."

That's fine, says the voice of reason. *Just make sure you schedule news time in the morning, afternoon, or early evening.*

"How early is *early*?" I ask.

Give yourself two hours of divisiveness-free time before going to sleep. You'll sleep better.

"I know from experience that this works better for me," I admitted, "but I don't often do it."

That's because, explained the irritatingly helpful voice of reason, *it is easier to keep replaying our habits even if we know they hurt us. It takes a little effort to change our habits. But once we institute a new habit in those last two hours of our day — a habit of doing tasks, having conversations, reading and seeing information that's uplifting — it becomes pleasant and quite easy.*

"But wait," I continue, "I wasn't actually watching the evening news, I was watching an entertaining late-night talk show that... well, satirized the news."

The same applies: if you want to sleep long and deep, don't watch anything on those shows that gets you mad or worried right before going to bed. Since you usually don't know what's coming in those shows, it's not so easy to avoid adrenaline-inducing divisiveness, unless you desist altogether.

"But I like watching those shows, and satirizing other people's divisiveness can be funny."

That's fine. You can have it both ways! You can sleep well and also enjoy any amount of divisiveness in full un-expurgated late-night political shows — just so long as you don't watch them late at night! It's a little scheduling adjustment. Watch them in the morning or afternoon or, if you have to, early evening.

When I succeed in desisting from playing the mouse caught in the glue-trap of a news habit, I do tend to sleep and feel better. Sometimes I watch late-night shows while I'm working out in the early morning. As for the evening, my rule — which I mostly follow, making exceptions for social and other reasons — is to make the last two hours before I go to bed kind of sacrosanct. Meaning that in those last two hours I avoid, so far as I can, churning my mind with divisive topics, and focus instead on things that are neutral, relaxing, and, if possible, uplifting.

EXERCISE

Protecting the Restfulness of Your Sleep

In the last two hours before going to bed, experiment with any or all of the following:

Actions to avoid

- Watching TV or internet programs that are divisive and may stoke worry, fear, anger, or *how-could-they!* reactions

- Reading books or articles that are divisive and may stoke worry, fear, anger, or *how-could-they!* reactions

- Watching or reading thrillers that increase your heart rate

- Watching or reading anything that riles or churns your mind

- Aerobic exercise, which increases adrenaline output — you know if your exercise is aerobic if it gets you out of breath. (On the other hand, aerobic exercise earlier in the day helps you sleep more deeply at night.)

Actions you can try

- Mental tasks that are relaxing

- Physical tasks that do not get you out of breath
  (i.e., are non-aerobic)

- Exercises that are centering or relaxing
  (e.g., gentle yoga, tai ji, relaxation techniques)

- Hobbies that don't require a computer screen

- Conversations with your loved one(s)

- Reading or listening to uplifting thoughts

- Playing or listening to relaxing music

- Writing down three things that happened that
  day that you are grateful for — especially effective
  when it's the last thing before bed.

If you are worried about the many things you need to get done (a worry that might carry into your sleep), list these many things, prioritize the list, and schedule your prioritized items in a time frame that's doable. At the very least, write down the list so that you don't go to sleep worrying about whether you might forget something that's important to you.

Reduce the Quantity of News Intake

News is supposed to be *new*, but when you listen to the news frequently, what you get is *olds*. You see and hear events repeated again and again, from different people and from slightly different angles. One news item can stretch over days, weeks, or months. When an important person comments on the news, this becomes news. And then when a second important person disagrees with the first important person, it is more news with an added touch of divisive drama. Your knowledge is hardly being expanded, but your outrage is, and of course outrage increases viewership, clicks, sales — and insomnia.

So, how do we make sure we learn what we need regarding what is going on, without getting hooked into repetition and continuing outrage? What is a healthy news diet? In experimenting with this, I found the following two steps very helpful.

1. Try a news fast for a week. If you don't need the news for your work, desist from seeing or hearing any news at all for seven whole days. Then, after a week, listen to the news and see what you missed. Most times, you won't have missed very much, because the same kind of stories repeat themselves, week after week — different nuances, different details, but usually the same characters and the same plot. The one-week news fast method helps wean you from dependence on the drama of the news that the news-media would — for financial reasons — prefer you to stay dependent on.

2. Then try a healthy news diet. For the longer-term, choose your medium of news reception and make sure you receive the news no more than once a day. Some people choose once a week, for instance via a weekly magazine. And some people choose less than that. Thomas Jefferson wrote, "I do not take a single newspaper, nor read one a month, and I feel myself infinitely happier for it." Henry Thoreau advised: "Read not the Times. Read the Eternities."

Of course, neither Jefferson nor Thoreau had smartphones. One of the hardest aspects of maintaining a healthy news diet may be handling the temptation of your smartphone.

The problem is that your smartphone is only about 1 percent phone. The other 99 percent is a complex distraction machine designed to tease you into as many clicks and links as possible. And not just randomly. That machine has already calculated exactly what distracts you the most, and goes for it, playing masterfully on your weaknesses, leading you inexorably to the advertisements it flashes before your eyes.

You might think, *Well, I can easily outsmart that phone by avoiding news items and by not reading any of those annoying ads.* But it's not called a smartphone for nothing. Sometimes, you pick up your phone to make a phone call—it seems a reasonable thing to do—but before you make the call, you've fallen headlong into the algorithmic fog of distraction. And then you find yourself reading some alarming news item or clicking on a dramatic link. Perhaps you don't even remember whom you were going to phone, or even that you were going to make a phone call at all.

Some people handle all this by using a landline for their phone calls. But for the majority who do not have landlines, we need to stay firm in the discipline of not slipping and sliding into our newsfeed (except at the times we designate). Good luck with that!

Or—and this may be a thousand times easier—disconnect your newsfeed. When I did this, I suddenly found I had more time in my day. And I was free of *breaking news* (news that breaks your concentration and good feeling).

Change the Tone of the Media You Access

If you don't want to suffer the turmoil, anger, and fear that come from imbibing divisiveness—with all the long-term damage it can cause to your mental and physical health—avoid divisive media. This is easy for me to recommend, but not so easy for most of us to put into practice because we tend to become addicted to the particular styles of drama that are plied by the channels we are used to.

Highly partisan news media create powerful drama that is super-tempting for many of us to watch. But it is almost impossible to come away from such newscasting without being riled by the awful things the other side has done.

It can be helpful to know who owns the news media you follow and whether the owner has a vested interest in portraying the news in a particular way or in trying to divide us in a particular direction. In 1960, the American journalist A. J. Liebling wrote:

> Freedom of the press is guaranteed
> only to those who own one.

This was true in 1960 and is more obviously true today. Since the acceleration of media mergers, most popular media is now in the hands of a very few media conglomerates, most of them owned or directed by a very rich person who effectively wields immense power of persuasion.

Media moguls tend to accumulate fortunes and are often more likely to support those politicians who offer them the biggest tax breaks and who are less likely to stop them from buying out competing media. Owners of media have the power to hire, direct, and fire any editor or writer they want—in this way, the owner's views become the views expressed by the media they own. In March 1997, for example,

Rupert Murdoch ordered the *Sun* newspaper in Britain to support Tony Blair—representing the more left-wing Labour Party—for prime minister, overriding the views of the *Sun's* editorial board, which had been consistently right wing and preferred the Conservative Party candidate, John Major. The editors had no choice if they wanted to keep their jobs.

Murdoch had a financial interest in Blair's winning and, therefore, in rousing his readers against the other contenders. In a British social science study that looked at the effects of Murdoch's directive, researchers estimated that the *Sun's* endorsement of Blair, forced by Murdoch's directive, were associated with approximately 525,000 extra votes for the Labour Party. Murdoch's prime motive, according to this research, was to protect his media companies at a time of government interest in breaking up media monopolies—something that Blair would not do. It seems that half a million people had changed their vote because it was in one man's financial interest for them to do so. The *Sun* did not, of course, explain to its readers the prime reason for its about-face from Conservative to Labour.

Knowing who controls the media you read and watch helps you to begin to fathom the bias that is coming your way. If someone offers you a drink, it's good to know if that person is a friend or an enemy. In the same way, it's good to know what the motives are of the person controlling the news you drink in, every day. What are they spinning and why?

Even when you have a sense of this kind of bias, however, it isn't easy to avoid being swayed by the divisive items you see or read. As human beings, our fear and anger responses bypass our intellect, and so it is easy to be seduced into taking sides—even with the intellectual understanding that there is likely to be bias. Added to this is another temptation: anger, for all its negative effects, can be exciting; and the drama can be addictively entertaining.

If it were just one or two short-lived dramas, no big deal. But divisive battles on the news go on and on, month after month, year after year, with little respite. And most of us suffer from our involvement with this constant divisiveness more than we might realize. It eats away at our peace of mind. There are many more innocuous choices we can make, for example, using media that:

- Do not support a particular political party or denigrate the opposing party

- Do not have an angry or divisive tone

- Give adequate sources for their information and try to present facts rather than just opinion

- Provide a more international voice.

In addition, I recommend that you check out who owns the media you take into your precious mind. What does the owner stand for? In what ways will his (at this time, media moguls are all men) desire for more market share influence the news he is willing to tell? You can change whom you follow, based on the results you find.

The media you choose can make a big difference to your peace of mind. Very few media meet all the criteria above—but there are some that meet most. When I was researching this topic, I tried Googling *media bias* and came across the *Media Bias Chart*. The Media Bias Chart is distinguished by the fact that pretty well no-one agrees with it. According to MarketWatch, this is because almost everyone thinks the media *they* choose is balanced. According to the Media Bias Chart's stated methodology, information is derived from rule-based analyses of individual articles and TV news sources, each rating carried out by three analysts with different political views (left, right, and center). How valid are these ratings? I cannot say, but seeing a whole spectrum of news sources in a visual, arranged according to possible bias, is food for thought.

Of course we tend to get pretty attached to the media we are accustomed to, but there's nothing stopping us from experimenting with new media, knowing that we can always change our minds.

If you do experiment with other media, it might be better to go cold turkey on the old one for at least a month. It's difficult to give the new a fair trial without dropping the old. If you end up choosing a more balanced voice, you will probably lose a certain amount of adrenalizing drama, but you might at the same time gain some equanimity. Which will you prefer?

CHAPTER 6

Protect Yourself from Divisive
Influences in Party Politics

A political party in a democratic country is a platform
on which to present and argue a particular point of
view, which the public can then review, determining
their vote based on an appraisal of the policies presented. *Ha ha.* Everyone knows things don't usually
work quite like this. In different countries, in different
centuries, politicians have recognized that the key to
public support is to approach the public through the
"emotional body"—i.e., what the public *feels* strongly
about. Gaining the "aye" of the emotional body is not
only more effective than arguing intellectually; it rec-
ognizes the fact that the emotional body often directs
the intellect.

It's useful, fun, and freeing to recognize the
games politicians play to snag their quarry. It frees
us from getting caught in a partisan, adrenaline-lad-

en battle. It can save us from getting dragged down into anger or hatred. With greater emotional freedom, we are better able to view policies that might be more helpful for us, for our country, and for posterity.

Here, then, are some examples of the games politicians play to get votes.

Votes by Otherizing

In chapter 2, I wrote of how politicians can gain adherents through otherizing: fomenting disapproval, anger, outrage, even hatred against the other side — or against a minority group with limited voting power. The great thing about looking through this lens is that it gives us a better chance to make a more informed choice. Here are four common diagnostic clues to demonstrate that a politician (or anyone else) is peddling otherization.

Clue #1: Overt Hostility

Sometimes politicians shout invective or screw up their faces in obvious expressions of anger, disgust, or blame. Emotions are highly contagious. If a politician raises his voice against others, it is easy to get the crowd into a similar mood. If you see old footage of Hitler screaming at Nazi Party rallies, you don't have to understand German to feel the waves of anger and hatred.

This kind of otherizing is, of course, obvious,

but that does not mean it isn't effective. Nor do you have to be unintelligent or uneducated to respond. Strong feelings of antipathy tend to rule the mind, no matter how well-educated we think we might be. The educated mind then gets used in service to the anger, providing rationalizations for why this anger is justified, reasonable, and even good: *Well, he's honest. He says it like it is... He's bold too... and he has my interest at heart... There really is a problem with those people—they are a threat to our way of life...*

Clue #2: Name-Calling and Judgment

One of the clearest symptoms of otherization is name-calling. Gangs, sects, tribes, nations, religions, and political parties call those who don't agree with them names that are differentiating, humiliating, or vilifying.

Name-calling has been used for millennia to disparage others with labels, which often stick. Christians and Muslims called those with different beliefs *heretics, pagans, infidels.* Any one of these words could become a sentence of death. The communists called the capitalists *capitalist pigs* or *the blood-sucking bourgeoisie,* while the capitalists called the communists *reds* or *commies.*

Some of the names may not sound so bad in themselves. *Commies,* for example, is just a shortened form of *communists*. But when descriptive terms have been used for years with connotations of derision and hatred, the terms themselves become shortcuts to separation and anger.

On the political party front, *Crooked Hillary* and *Moscow Mitch* are more modern examples of tying a leader to a disparaging label. The label may or may not contain objective truth, but if it is repeated often enough and laced with derision, it can separate the parties in escalating otherization.

Another telltale sign of otherizing is shifting the focus of attack from policy to the character of the policymaker. A policy can be criticized without otherizing the party that created it. But if the character of the person proposing the policy is judged, or the character of the whole party supporting the policy is derided, this is altogether different. Here are some common examples of blanket put-downs of people or groups we disagree with: *they're crazy; he's stupid; she's an idiot; they're a bunch of psychopaths; they're full of greed.* In addition to the obvious put-down and judgment, inherent in these examples is a wider dismissal of the person or group as being way lower on the scale of sanity, intelligence, morality, or humanity. Once the sanity, intelligence, morality, or humanity of the other camp has been sufficiently lowered, it is no longer necessary to listen to what they say.

Clue #3: Contempt

The politician builds a sense of grievance among his people by pointing the finger at what the other party — or the minority scapegoats — have done. What the other party is described as doing may be true, may be cherry-picked from past performance, may be exaggerated, or may be entirely made up. Any of these descriptions can then be juiced up with an otherizing dose of contempt.

The psychologist and mathematician John Gottman was able to predict whether newlyweds would stay married by watching a three-minute video of their interactions. His predictions were right in an astonishing 94 percent of cases. The most common factor that indicated likely future divorce was *contempt.* Contempt showed in putdowns, in eye-rolling and other easily discernible signs on the recorded videos.

Contempt, in Gottman's opinion, is like "sulfuric acid" to love. Rolling one's eyes might seem humorous — and, to be fair, it can be innocuously funny — but in response to a sincere comment from another, it is usually the body language of disdain or scorn. When we roll our eyes upward, the other becomes lower than our line of vision. Contempt is to hold oneself above the other person and, therefore, to consider the other as beneath oneself. *I am higher/you are lower* is a characteristic of otherization. By designating the other as beneath us, we are excluding them from the community of kinship and, so, from the natural openness of kindred compassion.

Just as contempt in a marriage predicts divorce, contempt in politics spells divorce from real conversation. Contempt can be expressed in several different forms of superiority, for example:

- Self-righteousness — *I'm right, you're wrong, and I'm morally superior to you.*

- Condescension — *I'm looking down at you from a superior intellectual height.*

- Patronization — *I'll try to explain it to you, you poor muddled thing.*

- Derision — *Compared to me, you are a piece of dirt.*

- Negative gossip — *Look what those idiots did!*

These forms of superiority are regularly used by members of both political parties in the U.S. Of course, the italicized statements on the attitude that is being expressed would rarely be admitted by the one who acts superior. Often, a superior attitude is not even recognized by the speaker as a put-down of the other. The ego, in its own interest, tends to disguise such self-knowledge — it just wouldn't feel good to admit to acting so obnoxiously. That being said, it is very easy for any of us, in politics or not, to fall into such forms of otherizing without realizing what we are doing.

Clue #4: Absolutes and Exaggerations

Most times, when we use the word *never*, we are exaggerating with an absolute, as in *you never care*. Actually, you probably do care sometimes. What we really mean is, *in my experience you often don't seem to care.*

But, isn't this just a way of speaking? Everyone knows you don't actually mean never!

Yes, it is a way of speaking, but at the same time this way of speaking creates divisive energy between *them* and *us*. As soon as anyone hears you say "you never...," their defenses go up, ready for battle. The reason for their defensiveness is that they've just been attacked (through exaggerating their badness) and they feel it.

On the positive side, absolutes and exaggerations spice our languages with drama and humor. In effective speeches, key points may be remembered because they have been painted with creative exaggeration. Good stories are embellished with the exaggerated deeds of demons and heroes. Cartoons and burlesques illustrate life's quirks and absurdities. And in terms of our learning, an exaggerated imitation of our foibles may help us recognize our blind spots; while deliberate exaggeration of an underused virtue can lead, over time, to the greater development of that quality. ☐

On the negative side, absolutes and exaggerations are used to accentuate divisions. To make their cases, politicians exaggerate the rightness of the view they support and exaggerate the wrongness of the view they fight against. These exaggerations can create black-and-white categories of right/wrong. Here are some examples of common words used as exaggerations to put down the other side:

COMMON ABSOLUTE OR EXAGGERATING WORDS	EXAMPLE ABOUT THEM	UNSTATED IMPLICATION ABOUT ME OR WE
Never	They *never* care.	*We care.*
All	They're *all* racists.	*We're not racists.*
Always	They *always* create divisions.	*We don't create divisions.*
Every	*Every* time they are in power, the economy tanks.	*The economy is good when we are in power.*
Only	She cares *only* about herself.	*I care about others.*
Absolute(ly)	He is *absolutely* wrong.	*I'm right.*
Entire(ly)	The *entire* institution is corrupt.	*We're decent.*
Complete(ly)	She *completely* misled us.	*I wouldn't do that.*
Nothing but	They're *nothing but* animals.	*I'm a good human being.*
Just	They're *just* devious.	*We're transparent.*
Downright	They're *downright* complicit in this.	*We're clean.*

Whenever you hear someone using the word "downright" in a critical statement about you, you can know that what they are probably saying is, *You are down and*

I am right. You will probably have noticed that the four means of otherizing described in the last few pages are not unique to politicians. If you read the comments on left-wing and right-wing blogs, the political otherizations made by party followers are often much more extreme. And outside of politics, probably all of us otherize at times.

All of us?

Perhaps.

Votes by Linking to Highly Emotive Issues

Advertisers often link their product to a strong emotion. The man who sees the ad of a beautiful woman sitting on the hood of a new car is quite aware that this woman is not going to improve visibility while driving; nor is she going to smooth the car's aerodynamic performance. But he is still more likely to buy the car. The advertiser's linking of an inanimate metal object to sexual desire works — amazingly — though few men would ever admit, or even realize, that the woman played any part whatsoever.

The U.S. Democratic Party did not support gay marriage until 2012 and then did support it. Historically, the Republican Party consistently voted to legalize greater access to abortion. Now, there is a strong move in the other direction. I doubt that many people think that these politicians suddenly changed their opinions through a deep process of moral contemplation. They made a 180-degree turn because they recognized that public opinion had altered enough to translate into some voting advantages. And, like successful advertisers, these politicians also recognized the importance of linking themselves to highly emotive issues. The seeming battle is on policy; the winner is often the one who wins the emotional body of the electorate.

Once an emotional issue has been chosen for voting advantage, the next task of the politician is to arm the emotional choice with extreme black-and-white thinking. Take the hot issue of abortion. Obviously, this is a complicated matter since the growing fetus is actually living inside another body. How can one determine the rights of each, especially if they are contradictory? The slogan for those who are more pro-abortion is "pro-choice," implying that the other side does not honor a woman's body or a woman's right to choose—in short, is misogynistic. The slogan for those who are more anti-abortion is "pro-life," implying that those on the other side are not only pro-death but murderers to boot.

There appears to be a complete impasse between these two extreme positions. Once positions become fixed into the emotional certainty of *we're right/ they're wrong, we're good/they're evil*, our ability to think things through plummets. For example, in all the fights between the two sides on this issue, the discussion of when the fetus becomes a human being is either rarely discussed or else discounted because it is assumed to be known categorically. Yet the time when we become a human being is crucial to determining whether abortion can be deemed "murder."

For those who do not believe in soul, the argument is a biological one. At what point, from an organism of a few cells and no brain, to a fish-like creature with gills, to a being of recognizable human form does the organism become a human being? Some believe that the fetus can be said to be a human being only when it is capable of sustaining life outside its mother's womb, while others believe the biological marker to be earlier.

For those who believe in soul, the question is a spiritual one: when does this soul first "enter" the body? Pretty well everyone agrees that the soul probably does not enter the sperm or ovum before they unite in conception. Otherwise masturbation by a male would be murder, and our prisons are already pretty full. Also, if the sperm and ovum both had souls, that could take male/female identity issues to another level of complexity.

Does the soul enter the body at the moment of conception? There is not a single reference in the Old Testament that would indicate this. The idea that the soul enters the body at conception is also not mentioned by Jesus or any of the New Testament writers. Because there is no biblical reference, the Catholic Church officially states that the time of ensoulment is unknown. At one point, the majority of Christians—following the teachings of two influential Christian saints, St. Augustine and St. Thomas Aquinas—believed that the soul enters the fetus at the time of quickening, when the mother first feels the baby kick at around four months. Why has this changed? Perhaps there are many reasons, but politics has played its part.

Different religions, politicians and social organizations have held different beliefs about the time of ensoulment—anywhere from the time of conception to the time of birth. Many of the beliefs are specific about the time after conception when ensoulment occurs—0 days, 40 days, 120 days, 134 days, 6 months, 9 months have all been put forward definitively by various religions, and by social or political groups. In 1978 psychologist Dr. Helen Wambach, in a series of documented group hypnosis sessions carried out over two years, hypnotized a total of 750 people, taking them back in time, it seemed, not only to before birth but to the point of ensoulment. All 750 people were asked to fill in a questionnaire about their experiences and the questions included, "When did you experience your soul joining the fetus?" Of the total, 89 percent said that their soul did not join with the fetus till after six months of pregnancy. Of these, 33 percent said that for them, ensoulment happened at birth.

Studies like this tend to get criticized because is not possible to prove that these pre-birth experiences are actual memories. But if they are not memories, we are still left with the surprising figure of 89 percent of subjects ending up with the belief that their ensoulment took place after six months of gestation. Most did not have these opinions before their hypnosis, and at no point in the hypnosis was any suggestion made about the time of ensoulment.

I am not saying that one should necessarily accept the views of these 89 percent. Nor am I saying that we should necessarily follow any one of the contradictory religious points of view about ensoulment as absolute truth. What I would like to suggest is that we don't know. When we start from the humbler point of not knowing what the right answer is, there is the possibility of real conversation. But politicians do not often seek conversation—they tend to seek side-taking and battle. Impassioned side-takers are more likely to vote.

Votes by Establishing a Strong Identity
The more politicians otherize opposition and emo-

tionalize issues, the more powerful the *us-and- them*, and the more we tend to identify with the *us*. For most U.S. politicians, the most successful identification is to get supporters to think *I am a Democrat* or *I am a Republican*. At this point, policies may hardly matter anymore, and some will vote in allegiance with "their" party for the rest of their lives, even if policies change drastically.

There is a big difference between saying *I am a Democrat* and *I choose to vote Democratic at this time*. The more we identify ourselves with a political party, the more we will tend to fit ourselves into whatever that party does, even if it is something that no longer suits our values. If we do not identify ourselves with a party, we may still decide to vote for a party as the better of two options, even if not everything suits our values. When we are not identified with a particular party, we have free choice in our decision: we are not caught in an automatic *this is who I am*.

The downside of identification with a party is that it reduces your intelligent discernment. If your very own self is identified with a political party, then a critique of "your" party feels like an attack on your very being. The *other* becomes the enemy and adrenalized anger easily follows. Which is why identity politics can be so dangerous.

Votes by Disguising Whom the Politician Really Serves

You know how race car drivers have ads written all over their driving suits, the size of the letters reflecting the amount of financial support received by the driver from the corporation being advertised? Well, suppose all politicians had to do the same, so it was publicly known who paid for their elections and with how much money.

The largest corporations have enormous power in U.S. politics—and in the politics of all democracies. Not only do these businesses own most of the media, they also, to a greater or lesser degree, own most politicians. Since Citizens United, under U.S. law corporations can now contribute unlimited funds toward the election campaign advertisements of those politicians whom these corporations support. Even though this is so well known—on a general level—individual politicians would risk losing the trust of at least some of those who voted for them if they became transparent about their private deals with powerful corporations.

Many measures that would be overwhelmingly popular among a politician's constituents do not happen simply because these politicians are more likely to try to please their corporate donors than they are their constituents. One long-term example is Medicare.

Unlike any normal company that can negotiate prices based on the volume of products bought, Medicare is, by law, not allowed to negotiate with pharmaceutical companies to lower drug prices—even though it is the largest single user of pharmaceutical products in the U.S. and could therefore massively lower drug costs! What this means, in effect, is that, because of laws passed by the U.S. Congress, the country's taxpayers are funding the pharmaceutical industry—even though the pharmaceutical industry has profit margins that dwarf those of the oil business. The public almost universally want drug prices and Medicare costs to go down, but no government, Republican or Democrat, has ever taken on the pharmaceutical lobby on this subject, even though they complain about Medicare costs. This is just one example of how large corporations control politicians' actions, even when these actions go against the peoples' needs and wishes. The pharmaceutical industry spent over $200 million lobbying politicians in 2018 and another $30 million on contributions to the election of the politicians who support them.

Healthy Detachment

When you are caught in the unpleasant divisiveness of party politics, it is still possible to detach yourself. *Detachment* is the ability—and willingness—to let go of (pre)conceptions and see things from a broader perspective. Detachment sometimes gets a bad press through confusion with aloof indifference. Detachment, in its best sense, does not mean being distant in the form of coldness; it does not involve being cut-off or lacking in empathy. On the contrary, detachment fosters care and compassion.

A visual analogy is to imagine two arguing parties of people divided by a partition. You are in one party, and you cannot see over the partition. You can only see your side of the situation, and your point of view is partisan, adrenalized, hot. But, if you could rise up, say in the basket of a hot-air balloon, and view the scene from above, you would then envision a wider picture, encompassing the various points of view. The partition would still be visible of course, but it would no longer obstruct your view of the whole situation. With this more elevated, more detached view, you have a greater chance of being fair and compassionate to both yourself and others. Detachment and compassion go together.

Detachment and intelligent action also go together. When you can see both sides of an issue more clearly, your wider vision increases your ability to act smartly and effectively.

EXERCISE

Rise above the *Us-and-Them* Game

In this exercise you will need to close your eyes through-out most of the steps — which makes it difficult to read them. I recommend audio if it is possible for you. You can either record steps 2 to 11 yourself and then listen to that recording, or, you are welcome to use my audio instruc-tions, free of charge by signing in to

doctorgillett.com/free-freakin-exercises

For this exercise, make sure you have alone time in a space you feel comfortable in. Or, you can do this exer-cise with a friend, or friends, and then compare notes af-terwards. If not required for emergency response, turn off all phones and other possible sources of electronic inter-ruption. Sit in a comfortable chair, and have a pen and a journal, notebook, or paper to write on.

The exercise takes less than ten minutes. Here is the writ-ten version of the steps.

1. Sit in a comfortable position.
2. Close your eyes.
3. Take a few deep breaths and relax.
4. Imagine yourself standing on one side of a field with all the people who agree with you. On the other side of the field, separated from you by a partition, stand

all the people who disagree with you. The two groups experience each other as enemies. You cannot see over the partition. Though you can hear people on the other side of the partition saying things you disagree with. You strongly argue your point of view.

5. Be aware of how you feel in this situation.

6. In a moment, I'm going to ask you to allow yourself to disassociate from your own point of view. To do this, imagine that you actually jump out of your own body, so to speak. Your body remains where it was, arguing away, while your mind's eye floats upwards... till it is hovering at about 30 feet. You are completely safe up here. In your mind's eye, you can see your body beneath you, arguing away. But even though you can see yourself doing this, you are not emotionally involved. You observe yourself with kindness.

7. From your new height, your whole perspective is changed. You can see the partition between the two arguing groups. You can see that the two groups of people are stuck behind the partition and cannot really see each other's viewpoints, or see a higher view. But you can see both groups. You notice how similar they are. You recognize that, at the most basic level, all the people, on both sides of the partition, want the same things: happiness, kindness, a good living, security, appreciation. They all have families; they want the best for their families. They all like to laugh and to feel self-respect...

8. You see yourself beneath you, and you too are similar in all these wishes.

9. Be aware of how you feel, as you see yourself and see these two groups with all their similar wishes and feelings.

10. When you're ready, allow your point of consciousness to float downward slowly, until it joins your body once again. Only now you are changed because you take with you your vision of all the people on both sides being so very similar in their needs, wishes, and humanity.

11. Now, open your eyes. Write down your experience. What happened for you? How did you feel?

Doing this exercise, you may find yourself, at least for a time, above the political fray—not "above" in the sense of superior, above in the sense of seeing more clearly and with more compassion and kindness. By writing down your experience, you help ingrain this stance, so that it becomes easier to take a higher perspective in the future.

CHAPTER 7

The Pleasure of Dropping Anger, and How to Do It

You know how when you read or hear about a new drug, it is hyped as having a particular beneficial effect and this is then followed by a host of potential side effects displayed

in tiny print, or on TV in an incredibly fast, quiet, bland, and unemotional voice.

Quite often, the last item on the list of possible side effects is

death.

Our own emergency secretions of adrenaline, cortisone, and other fight/flight hormones can be seen as internal drugs with a history of millions of years. The prime positive effect is that these natural drugs prepare your body to be maximally efficient in physical reactions of emergency fight or flight. Some of the side effects are:

> Addiction to anger, addiction to the excitement of emergency; loss of pleasure and contentment; sleeplessness; increased muscle tension; increased tension between self and others; the creation of an "at war" footing that may have permanent repercussions (e.g., war); others reacting to you with anger or fear; loss of accurate discernment; poor decision making; diminished intelligence while angry; loss of ability to empathize or feel compassion; loss of ability to reach across to the other side; loss of ability to experience and engage curiosity; loss of ability to experience respect and to act with kindness; extreme contagiousness of the inflammation of anger from person to person, or from a media source to multiple people; indigestion; diminished immune response; increased likelihood of infection and cancer; long-term association with increased morbidity; and long-term association with early death.

The good news is that it is possible to vastly diminish our angry reactions, if we would like to, and our lives are usually happier when we do so.

No One Else Can *Make* You Angry

The Greek philosopher Epictetus said, "When anyone makes you angry, know that it is your own thought that has angered you." This quote gets people really angry—which, of course, according to the quote, is impossible!

The idea that *it is your own thought that has angered you* is not just provocative—it is deeply empowering.

When we fully take in the fact that other people do not actually have the power to control our emotional state, we are liberated from dependency on what others do. This is true freedom.

But wait a minute... Isn't it natural to get angry when someone with power makes a decision that hurts people! When people die because of a tyrant's desire for power! When the rich get richer and the poor get poorer! Look at all the awful things that are happening in this world through the actions of some of those in power! Surely, it's natural to be angry at such things.

Yes, it's natural, and I'm offering no judgment on the ensuing anger—yours or my own. But there is a way to move through it. We don't need to suffer the multiple side-effects of anger with its damage to our clarity of thought and its long-term deleterious effect on our health.

But what about the damage caused by repressing anger. I've heard that repressing anger can lead to depression and many other conditions.

I am not advocating repression. I am advocating being clear about our anger and then finding the root cause of the anger: this defuses the anger. The anger is neither repressed nor expressed—it is dissolved!

OK, but why would we want to dissolve it? What about the positive effects of anger? Doesn't anger drive change? Angry people demand something different. The energy of anger can get people together to fight to make a better world.

The most overtly angry people I've heard about on the news are suicide-bombers. Does their anger improve their cause? No. It turns the world against them. And what about the generations of African Americans who had plenty of reason for anger at the centuries of discrimination, cruelty, and enslavement? Did their overt anger, when occasionally expressed in violence, improve their situation? No, it created a re-action of fear and counter-anger and turned a major-ity of white people even more against them. Without doubt, the most significant beneficial changes in law and in representation in government occurred after the courageous nonviolent revolution by Martin Lu-ther King and hundreds of thousands of other Afri-can Americans.

OK, but what about anger expressed without physical violence. Can't that draw people together to fight for a cause?

Yes, it can. But still, when we experience long-term anger over a cause, we ourselves suffer mentally and physically.

Well, isn't that worth it if the cause is just?

No, because there are other ways, besides anger, of motivating people to fight together for a cause. In fact, an angry stance tends to be less successful in the long run. You don't *have* to be poisoned with the inner drugs of emergency and alarm; you can fight courageously, and often more effectively, without them.

This is hard to believe. How can fighting with anger be less effective? You have to agree that anger is energizing.

Yes, anger is energizing. But in what direction? And with what results? If a Democrat expresses anger by vilifying a Republican (in the hope of uniting Democrats and their supporters), the Republican(s) will likely retaliate. Anger creates anger back. This is pretty much automatic. It is almost as inevitable as Newton's third law of motion: *Any action has an equal and opposite reaction.* This law seems to apply to e-motion as well as to motion—even if the math is not quite so measurable. If a Republican expresses anger by vilifying a Democrat (hoping to unite Republicans and their supporters), the Democrat(s) will similarly tend to react in kind. In these ways, the divide increases, and getting things done becomes more and more difficult. Anger is fundamentally divisive. This is true whether it is expressed overtly in insults or a little more covertly in contempt or in righteous-sounding outrage.

OK, I can see the pitfalls, but isn't it also true that divisive, angry leaders have been phenomenally successful at getting people to unite in anger? Hitler is a prime example. I'm not advocating this of course, but it seems like a scary truth.

In the short term, unfortunately, and undeniably, proclaimed anger and hatred can work in uniting a group against another group—through the exploitation of human foibles. But long-term, it never works. Martin Luther King wrote: "History is cluttered with the wreckage of nations and individuals that pursued this self-defeating path." Hitler's initially "successful" actions created a reaction from other nations that destroyed everything he built. Though it took some years.

Well, if you don't use anger, how then do you unite people for a good cause?

Passion.

Passion?

Yes, passion for the result you want. Passion for kindness, for example. Passion for equal opportunity. Passion for equal pay for men and women doing the same jobs. Your emotional energy is not primarily aimed divisively against those who obstruct your vision—which will only serve to increase their obstruction. It is primarily aimed (non-divisively) at your positive vision for the future. You don't *lack* emotional energy when you are not angry; you *direct* your emotional energy into your dream of how things can be.

This sounds fine, but how do you get rid of the anger you already have?

The first thing is to recognize that no one can ever *make* you angry. If you think another person can *make* you angry, you have given that person power over you. In other words, your anger is actually a form of dependency. But when you drop this belief that someone else can make you angry, you are in charge of your own state. Consider the joy of accepting that no-one, ever, can control your emotional state. Think of the freedom this will bring you. Your happiness is no longer under the control of what other people say or do!

That sounds great, but my anger happens so automatically, it doesn't feel like I have a choice. When a political leader lies, for example, I get angry. It doesn't seem like it's my decision.

So, why are you angry when a political leader lies?

Well, obviously, because he lied.

Are there times when the same political leader lies just as badly, and you are not angry?

Yes.

Then there must be something in you that determines whether you get angry or not.

That's logical.

Yes, and it's true. The key to gaining decision-making power over our anger is to recognize the cause within us. Anger—when it is not in direct reaction to physical threat—is caused internally by a strong expectation or need we have that is not being met. To use your example, if you can take *I'm angry because you lied...* and shift it to *I'm angry because of my own need for trust...* an amazing thing happens: the anger begins to abate.

Why?

Because you have taken your attention away from the person who lied, and switched your attention to your own needs — and these include the universal human needs for qualities like trust, respect, and integrity. So, you might say, *I am angry because of my need for integrity, respect, and trust.* This means you are no longer focused on an enemy. You have become focused on your own needs and personal values. When there is no enemy in your mind, the anger goes. And then, the shift of focus to your own needed values opens you to the more elevated feelings of peacefulness, courage, and compassion.

You have shifted from the negative to the positive. And you have also shifted from the external — over which you have no control — to the internal, which is within your own circle of power. You cannot *make* your need for respect and trust be fulfilled by a politician you've never met. But you can fulfill those same needs in other ways.

EXERCISE

Overcoming Anger

If you are angry with a person — or with a group or a political party — for something they have said or done, and
if you have no way to change the outcome of their behavior or to give them meaningful feedback, I invite you
to do this exercise to overcome your anger. The exercise
is derived from sources some two thousand years old, in
addition to the more recent practice of Non-Violent Communication as taught by Marshall Rosenberg. For more
detail, see the endnotes.

The exercise requires your undivided attention, so it's great
to do this exercise at a time when you know you will not
be interrupted. Make sure you have a pen and paper (or
notebook) ready, and sit in a comfortable chair in a private
space. The exercise takes anywhere from 5 to 20 minutes.

1. The first task is to recognize your anger, which may
   not always be obvious to you:

   - It may be apparent only at night, when
     you are less guarded.

   - It may manifest in body language: in your facial
     expression, tight forearms (the muscles that
     make fists), or tightness in any muscles of
     action — legs, abs, back, shoulders, neck.

- The anger may be muted in irritation, annoyance, impatience, resentment, judgmentalism, blaming, or complaining.

- It may be ice-cold, as in hatred or calculated revenge.

- It might also manifest in various forms of covertly aggressive superiority such as condescension, patronization, derision, sarcasm, contempt.

- If your anger is hidden or disguised in one of these ways, allow yourself to be open with your anger in a safe place. By a *safe place* I mean a space in which your anger will not cause you or anyone else harm. Examples are journaling *I feel angry because...* or, in the privacy of your own room, expressing your anger by yelling or hitting pillows with your fists. These practices do not get rid of anger. The purpose is simply to witness and acknowledge the extent of your anger and to begin the process of acceptance of yourself as you are.

2. Once you have recognized your anger, be kind to yourself.

   - Please do not judge yourself for having anger in any of its many forms.

   - Remember that there is nothing wrong with anger in itself. Anger is only problematic to us when we cannot move beyond it, and it is only a problem to others if we express our anger in violent words or actions. Take your anger as a sign of your being (probably) human, and as an invitation to explore and to learn.

- If judgmental thoughts about yourself come up, there is no need to judge your judgments — simply observe them with kindness.

- If pain underlies your anger (as it often does), acknowledge your own pain with kindness.

3. With regard to the others' words or actions that relate to your anger, ask yourself: what was my expectation (how I think the world ought to be) that was not fulfilled? Write down the answer and allow yourself to be uncensored. For example: "He should have been honest... Politicians should tell the truth — they should not lie to maintain their power."

4. Remind yourself that you have no control over what someone else says or does. Recognize that your expectation of how things should have gone is actually out of touch with reality. Why? Because in reality it did not happen. (And some politicians *do* lie.)

5. Now ask yourself: *What is my personal need that was not met by these things I cannot control?* Write down the answer. And if you can't think what your need might be, see if any of the following examples of universal needs fits for you:

SOME UNIVERSAL NEEDS (OR HIGHLY VALUED QUALITIES OF BEING)			
Authenticity	Courage	Independence	Respect
Choice	Ease	Integrity	Safety
Clarity	Effectiveness	Joy	Security
Community	Equality	Kindness	Tolerance
Compassion	Harmony	Order	Trust
Competence	Inclusion	Peacefulness	Truthfulness

6. Write down: *I feel angry because of my need for...* (complete this statement with one or two personal needs that you come up with or choose from the chart above.) The internal need must relate only to you and not to any other person. For example, *I feel angry because of my need for trust,* and not... *because of my need for this political leader to tell the truth.* The former gives me full power for my own state, while the latter makes me continue to be dependent on the actions of another person.

7. This next step requires you to close your eyes. So please read through the instructions in the bullet points below a few times till you have the gist of what you will do, and then close your eyes.

   • Focus on the need for one of the qualities that you wrote down in step 6.

   • Imagine that this quality is held gently in your heart.

   • Enjoy the feeling of this quality.

   • Imagine yourself manifesting this quality or expressing this quality with others.

8. Open your eyes and write down what happened for you.

9. Write down one way you can take personal action to augment the quality you feel you need. This action should be one that is doable by you alone (and does not involve any reliance on another person or another situation to change).

10. Schedule and practice the practical action you chose.

I found that doing this just once did not stop my being angry again. I guess this is not surprising. I did, however, find that repeating the exercise made it easier and easier to defuse my own anger.

It is a personal accomplishment to overcome your own anger without either repressing it or expressing it in violent words. Good luck with your experiments in anger dissolution! Enjoy the empowering game of discovering the source (and therefore the solution) within yourself!

CHAPTER 8

Handle Others'
Anger Brilliantly

In any person-to-person confrontation, it is perhaps astonishing that as soon as we drop our own anger, the anger of the other side usually diminishes. This is because of a truth that pretty well everyone has experienced: anger leads to anger back; judgment leads to judgment back. These cycles easily escalate.

Conversely, when there is a genuine absence of angry reaction, the anger of the other tends to subside: on an emotional level, there's nothing to hit back at.

On a larger social scale, the same is true. Anger and judgment on one side create anger and judgment on the other side in a vicious cycle of escalating divisiveness. It is difficult for most of us to break out of such a situation, because our anger always seems (to us) warranted by what the other side did.

Martin Luther King was a master at interrupting the vicious cycle of anger that he encountered in the 1950s and '60s. African Americans had a lot to be angry about — for example, the denial of equal rights, segregation written into law, hate based on prejudice, the Ku Klux Klan, and eighty years of lynchings. But despite all this, King and those who marched with him disciplined themselves to show no anger or violence. The result was that most of the violence was perpetrated by their white-skinned oppressors.

In 1963, Theophilus Eugene ("Bull") Connor, the commissioner of public safety in Birmingham, Alabama, infamously ordered dogs and fire hoses to be turned on children who were demonstrating peacefully for equal rights. When the American public saw television scenes of African American children being attacked by dogs and knocked down and swept away by the powerful water jets from fire hoses, many were appalled: it was the white-skinned people who were manifesting uncivilized violence. The contrast between the peaceful demonstrators and the violence of those trying to stop them had a powerful effect. President Kennedy once commented wryly to King: "The civil rights movement owes Bull Connor as much as it owes Abraham Lincoln."

Bull Connor's order for violence was ultimately beneficial for the civil rights movement only because

Martin Luther King and company refused to play the game of retaliation. There had been hundreds of Bull Connor act-alikes since the end of slavery in the U.S., but a majority of Americans had excused or turned a blind eye to these violent discriminatory actions because they held the extreme otherizing view that African Americans were morally inferior beings. King and his followers, brilliantly, turned this belief on its head by demonstrating that the non-violent African Americans acted with clear moral superiority compared to the violent, white-skinned suppressors of equality. Everyone could see this on television. Though this was not the end of racial prejudice, things could never be the same again.

Refusing to show anger was a brilliant tactic, quite apart from its moral lessons, because it was this that truly began to break the age-old cycle of anger creating further anger, judgment creating judgment, hatred creating more hatred. And though it did not end prejudiced thinking, it *was* highly effective, leading to major changes in U.S. law—the Civil Rights Act of 1964 and the Voting Rights Act of 1965.

Despite the documented success of such methods—King and Mahatma Gandhi's nonviolent movements are stand-out examples—the temptation to retaliate against insult is so immediate and feels so "right" that we often go ahead without considering the consequences. We might be aware, intellectually, that it's not generally a good idea to escalate the anger coming at us, but then, in the heat of the moment, the intellect is somehow bypassed by our adrenalized reaction. Have you ever written an email in reaction to an insult, thought you were being pretty cool and reasonable, and then, a few days later—when you actually *were* cool and reasonable—reread what you wrote and realized how hot your reply really was?

The temptation to respond to perceived anger in kind, but not in kindness, happens in all sorts of situations: in personal relationships—for instance, spousal retaliation escalating into spousal war—in work situations, in political situations. In U.S. party politics, the emotional tit-for-tat has escalated into derision so deeply felt that real bipartisan conversation between politicians, and even between voters, has become very difficult.

So, what do you do when there is anger or insult coming at you—whether it's in-person, on the phone, or via the news? If you wish to avoid your own angry reaction, consider these three levels to handling another's anger:

1. Pause. Avoid expressing your own immediate angry reaction, which prevents the mutual escalation of anger in the moment. You may or

may not decide to give your response when the adrenaline surge has ebbed away.

2. Defuse your own anger.

3. Find empathy by understanding why the other is angry.

Level 1: Pause

Avoid expressing your angry reaction immediately, in order to prevent the mutual escalation of anger. This rule of thumb is often recommended, but not always so easy to follow when communications are hot.

Pausing is useful when you are in the presence of an angry person or people—and also when you encounter anger in writing or on social media. Here are some more specific thoughts about each of these two situations.

When you are in the presence of an angry person or people

- Pause.
- Don't speak.
- Take a deep breath.

Your deep breath should be quiet, private. I've seen someone take a deep breath in a hot situation and then exhale with the sibilant sound of a hissing snake: this did not reduce the other person's anger. Taking a deep breath interrupts our automatic, adrenaline-driven, fight/flight reaction. One of the physiological mechanisms of this useful means of self-management is that a deep breath stimulates the vagus nerve, which slows down the speeding heart.

Many people owe their lives to this simple maneuver of pausing. The evidence for this is in the number of people who *didn't* pause and are now dead. In the U.S., the most common reason for homicide is to finish an argument—with a rather high degree of finality—about who is right and who is wrong. Arguments about who is right and who is wrong account for some 30 percent of murders in the U.S., and this motive for murder is more common than any other—for instance, murders committed in the pursuit of theft, rape, or narcotics-related crime.

When you encounter anger in writing or on social media

- Pause.
- Don't write an angry email or text—or if you do write it, don't send it.
- Don't promulgate anything insulting on social media.

Remind yourself that your intelligence is severely diminished when you are angry or upset. The adrenaline response actually shuts down neurons in your intelligent forebrain, making rational thought difficult or impossible. Pausing does not mean you won't take action. It means that whatever action you take will come after a period of cooling off—which gives a chance for the neurons in your forebrain to reconnect.

Level 2: Defuse Your Own Angry Reaction

After you have succeeded in not escalating the anger through avoiding the immediate expression of your own anger, the next task is to *defuse* your anger. To do this, you can follow the exercise "Overcoming Anger" in chapter 7.

As soon as you can fully recognize that your anger is internally caused through the frustration of your own expectations, and you can acknowledge your own needs, your blame of the other person or people disappears, and the anger (which is basically a physiological protective mechanism against an enemy) disappears in proportion to the diminishing blame.

Level 3: Find Empathy by Understanding Why the Other Is Angry

The third level is to look for the cause of the anger in the other person or people. It's not that we will definitely *find* the cause of their anger, but in even attempting this exploration and making a reasonable guess, we can usually find the beginnings of empathy in ourselves.

In 1996, I attended a week-long workshop with Dr. Marshall Rosenberg. Rosenberg was a psychologist, the founder of Nonviolent Communication (NVC), and a travelling peacemaker. Brought up in the 1940s in Detroit, Michigan, Rosenberg as a young boy witnessed race wars in which many were killed, and he himself was frequently beaten up on his way to school for having inherited a Jewish surname. These experiences, he said, catalyzed his quest to try to understand judgment, violence, and compassion. Over the years, he created a system of communication designed to by-pass judgment and create empathy. He taught this system in more than forty different countries, including war-torn regions of the world like the Middle East, Croatia, Serbia, Ireland, Rwanda, and Burundi.

When I met Rosenberg, he was in his seventies: tall with a chiseled face; gray, wiry hair; and a wicked sense of humor. In fact, he was such a comedian that the whole group would burst into guffaws of laughter at his wit and good humor. He had a gift of being able to guide people into finding empathy even in the most emotionally charged and hate-filled scenarios. Sometimes he would illustrate his points with stories from the past. I listened with attention when he chose as one of his illustrations the long-standing conflict between Israel and Palestine. I thought, *If someone can find genuine empathy in a situation like that, anything must be possible.*

Rosenberg had been invited to teach Nonviolent Communication in a public meeting in a Palestinian refugee camp in Bethlehem. Because he was an American and had a name like Rosenberg, this was not an easy assignment. Only the day before, Rosenberg had noticed some spent tear-gas canisters in the refugee camp with *Made in the USA* clearly marked on them. He knew that the refugees were angry with the U.S. for siding with Israel and supplying them with tear-gas and other weapons of control or destruction.

When Rosenberg walked into the makeshift meeting room, he saw 170 glowering, murmuring men. "You murderer!" one of them shouted. "Assassin!" another yelled. "Child-killer!"

This was not going to be an easy audience. Rosenberg, remembering the tear-gas canisters, spoke to the man who had first called him a murderer. "Sir, are you feeling upset because you would like my government to act in a different way?"

"That's right," the man said fervently. "We don't need tear gas. We don't need your bombs. What we need is schools, health clinics, housing. We need to be able to take care of our children."

"Sir, it sounds like you're feeling desperate for the world to know the kind of situation you are living in."

"That's right. My children go to a school with no books. Not a single book! My son is sick. He plays in open sewage because there is nowhere for him to play. Have you ever seen kids playing in open sewers?"

"It sounds like you want for your children to have what any parent would want for their children..."

At the end of the presentation, the Palestinian man who had called Rosenberg a murderer invited him to have Ramadan dinner with his family.

This snippet of a much longer conversation demonstrates one man's mastery in handling another's anger. First, Rosenberg does not express any angry or fearful reaction to being called a murderer. Secondly, though it is not explicit in this condensed version of the conversation, he is able to defuse any emotional reaction he might have had—which is why he is open and can show genuine empathy to the Palestinian man. And thirdly, he discovers the need behind the Palestinian man's anger. In doing this, Rosenberg takes the conversation from divisive anger into the arena of universal needs—"what any parent would want for their children." That which divides is transported to the arena of that which unites.

The following exercise is based on Marshall Rosenberg's method of Nonviolent Communication.

EXERCISE

Find Empathy by Understanding Why the Other Is Angry

- Recognize that the other person's anger, just like your own, is nearly always created by an unmet need or value.

- State the feeling that you observe in the other. If the feeling you observe is something that might be viewed in a negative light — something like, for instance, *anger* or *jealousy* — you can soften this by using more easily acceptable words, like *annoyed* or *upset.* ("Are you feeling upset because…" Marshall Rosenberg asked the man who had called him a murderer.) People feel seen and heard when you demonstrate that you've noticed what they feel, even if they need to correct your guess at this feeling — *no, I'm not feeling annoyed so much; I'm feeling more unhappy.* If you don't quite capture the feeling as the other experiences it, your guess at their feeling still demonstrates your care.

- Link the feeling that you have observed (or that they have named) to an underlying need/value they hold that is not being met. Ask yourself, *what is this person's human need or value that is not being met?* Make your best guess at this, even if you feel the other person is not themselves aware that this is a problem for them. Then link this need/value to the feeling you have identified. Put your two linked guesses in the form of a question like this: *Are you upset because you would like peacefulness and harmony?* Here is a list (the same as in the last chapter) of some universal human needs/values:

SOME UNIVERSAL NEEDS (OR HIGHLY VALUED QUALITIES OF BEING)			
Authenticity	Courage	Independence	Respect
Choice	Ease	Integrity	Safety
Clarity	Effectiveness	Joy	Security
Community	Equality	Kindness	Tolerance
Compassion	Harmony	Order	Trust
Competence	Inclusion	Peacefulness	Truthfulness

- Recognize that you probably have the same needed values.

- Watch the anger cycle diminish as you experience your commonality with the other.

In a personal relationship, you are likely to find that you're able to discuss your guess of the other's feeling and need/value fairly easily. For example, after an argument of harsh words and hurt, you might say, *Are you feeling upset because you would like to experience kindness?* This question is so disarming! In asking a question like this, you do not need to be exactly right.

With the question, you are creating an opening. You are switching from battle mode into the language of universal needs and values. Everyone wants to experience kindness.

And if the other person is a public figure, or a public group (members of a political party, for example), your guess, made internally for your own benefit, can still be very useful in reducing your own pain and judgment. Even attempting to guess the need behind another's anger, tends to diminish your own judgmental or angry response. This is because you are moving from *divisiveness* (us-versus-them, anger with the enemy) to *unity* (the wishes and needs that are universally valued).

Democrats and Republicans often judge each other for voting for the other side, with irrational, blanket putdowns — irrational because the blanket casts all members of the other camp as the same, not taking into account that the reasons for voting are complex and may be different in different voters.

Perhaps an important need of a particular man who voted Republican is for fairness and security — for example, to feel that he can properly support his family after forty years in which wages for most of the 99 percent have not increased in real terms. Perhaps an important need for a particular woman who voted Democratic is for fairness and equality — for example, that women receive equal pay to men for equal work.

In making the other into a person, it's easier not to be hurt by labels hurled with pain, like "Republicans are a bunch of racists" or "Democrats are a bunch of self-righteous idiots." Dropping the labels and counter-labels, we see people like you and me who share the same basic human attributes, like, for instance, caring about family, wishing to be appreciated, loving to laugh, enjoying good food, wanting to be heard…We see that they, like us, share the same desire for trust, for warmth, for having fun, for making a contribution, for self-expression, for purpose, for safety, for independence, and for respect. And in recognizing our commonality, we feel so much better.

The more we experience our common ground, the more we find that enmity evaporates, and the better we become at reaching out to those with different views.

CHAPTER 9

Decide What Is within Your Own Power

There is great relief in clearly delineating what is within your power to achieve — and what is not. You see things happening that you would like to change. Some things you really can change, and some things you cannot.

If the change you would like to see involves anyone else at all, then it is not within your power to *make it happen* — since other people have choices that you cannot control. This does not, of course, mean that you shouldn't ask another person to make a change. It's just that you have no guarantee that the other person will do what you want.

And if the change you would like to see involves the doings of the physical universe (including your physical body), it is also not in your power to *make it happen*, since you do not, unless you are very unusual, have the power to make the universe obey you.

In short, you have definitive control only over your own thoughts, words, and actions. You can vote, you can encourage others to vote, you can also "vote" through what you buy or don't buy, you can take part in demonstrations, voice your opinions, write to your political representative... But you cannot, unless you are a dictator in a pretend-democracy, control the result of the election.

Having such clarity is helpful. Recognizing what is outside your sphere of control gives tremendous relief from the burden of carrying national situations on your shoulders. This reduces tension. It diminishes that hopeless feeling that can arise from seeing a problem as an unscalable mountain of complexity that daunts you into helplessness and inaction. Paradoxically, by recognizing that you cannot guarantee the broad changes you would like, you are then free to focus on the real changes that you can accomplish.

E Comes before D

Knowing that we have control over our actions, but not over the results of our actions, reduces the anger and disappointment that arise from unmet expectations. Expectation precedes Disappointment. Or, as Benjamin Franklin put it, "Blessed is he who expects nothing, for he shall never be disappointed."

But, wait a minute, isn't it good to expect good things? Isn't this a mark of optimism, and doesn't optimism create both increased opportunities and happiness?

Yes, expectation in the sense of general optimism and hopefulness is very helpful. The problem occurs when expectation contains insistence on our exact vision manifesting. When there is demand in our expectation, we become emotionally bound to our expectations coming to pass in the way we want and according to our timeline.

Appointments

How can we be sure there is demand in our expectation? Easy. The clue is disappointment. For some, this disappointment is experienced more as hurt, for others more as anger—or sometimes it's a mixture of the two. When there is no demand in our expectations, we do not feel bad when our vision does not manifest in the way—and in the time—we expected. When there is some demand that things *should* come out the way we want, on the other hand, we feel a keen disappointment when they don't. We have made an *appointment* in our own minds with an imagined result, with a destiny we cannot control. When this appointment is not met by reality, we feel the pang of *dis-appointment*. Our imaginary *appointment* has been *dis*-sed by reality. We blame life for not conforming to our wishes, and we feel pain, not realizing that this pain comes from the appointment that we ourselves pre-constructed in our minds. When friends, family, or society in general all share the same expectations, it makes it even harder to let go of them.

Freedom from these boxes of expectation creates contentment.

But, hey, does this mean we sit back and do nothing in zombiesque recline, acquiescing to whatever life brings?

Not at all. We can work hard for what we want, without handcuffing ourselves to a particular result that may be beyond our control—for example, any result that depends on what others do or don't do! Freedom, say the wise ones, is not being emotionally attached to the results of one's actions. It does not mean not acting.

Here is a simple and effective exercise to help reduce the burden of carrying disappointment with the way things have worked out (at this present time) socially and nationally.

EXERCISE

Clarifying Power and Action

1. Write down something that, ideally, you would like to see happen, something important to you. This is a statement of what you dearly wish for and does not need to be something that is within your power to make happen.

2. Now, make a list of things you would like that *are* within your power to do, things that might help achieve what you want from step 1 — though there are no guarantees.

3. Decide which of the items from list 2 you *choose* to do. Circle or highlight these.

4. Schedule actions on the items you've chosen.

5. Perform these scheduled actions, remembering that results cannot be guaranteed. Take pleasure in making your best effort.

CHAPTER 10

The Liberating Power of Curiosity

Curiosity is an innate feature of being human. Curiosity is the impulse that delights a baby in the unbridled exploration of touch and taste and scent. It is the drive to discover; it is the quest to question *why* until we reach a satisfying answer or a deeper question; it is a key to learning with joy. Great leaps forward in human understanding—from medicine to motor vehicles, from molecular structure to the motion of planets—have occurred as the result of people's curiosity. Isaac Newton, Marie Curie, and Albert Einstein were famously curious about this world and how it works. "The important thing is not to stop questioning," Einstein said, "...never lose a holy curiosity." Einstein, in fact, claimed that he had no special talents, but that he was "passionately curious." The statesman and philanthropist Bernard Baruch wrote of Newton: "Millions saw the apple fall, but Newton asked why."

Why, one might ask, doesn't the apple fall sideways?

Conventional understanding might reply, *That's just how things are. Things fall downward. Don't question it.*

Curiosity asks, *But why?*

The essence of curiosity is open-mindedness—being willing to question, and being willing to admit we don't know the answer.

Curiosity helps us challenge our own assumptions about the world and other people.

I wonder if that's really true? Could there be another explanation?

Because curiosity is by nature open and non-judgmental, it is a wonderful antidote to otherizing. Curiosity stays in the realm of objectivity; it is a fascination with what might be, not a fastening to a cause. Curiosity evaporates fixed judgments; it delights in observing, wondering, discovering, playing with the multiple strands of possibility. Compare, for example, the following statements of curiosity and judgment:

SITUATION	STATEMENT OF CURIOSITY	STATEMENT OF JUDGMENT
Responding to an idea one disagrees with	*I wonder why she thinks that.*	*She's an idiot!*
Responding to an action one disagrees with	*I wonder why he does that.*	*He's an idiot!*
Responding to a political act of violence that kills innocent people	*I wonder why they are so angry.*	*They're just terrorists; they should be exterminated!*

In each situation, curiosity leads to the possibility of greater understanding, and in some cases dialogue, while judgment is a closed declaration of derision and separation. Judgment turns the judged into an inferior other, someone unworthy of further consideration. Curiosity opens. Judgment shuts.

In addition to opening our minds, curiosity also helps us converse with others with greater openness. Books on the art of conversation explain that one of the key skills in overcoming awkwardness, shyness, or self-absorption is to be genuinely curious about the other person, to be interested in why he thinks as he does, why she made those particular choices.

Despite the great benefits of curiosity, which has enabled every human advance in understanding, this quality is not universally valued. In fact, it's received some pretty bad press. Some people confuse curiosity with prying—for example, delving into the personal lives of the rich and famous.

We are told that curiosity killed the cat. But the name of that cat was Ignorance.

The idea that curiosity killed the cat was used to warn the curious about the dangers of exploration. But exploration requires searching, not recklessness. Perhaps the real danger of curiosity is that it can examine beliefs that people hold as absolute truth, and this can create an angry reaction. Some are afraid that curiosity may question social views and party lines. It knocks at the door of every box we've put someone in, and sometimes we prefer to keep those doors closed.

When a curious child asks, *why?... but why?... but why?* do her parents get annoyed, or do they celebrate the fact that her curiosity is still alive? For many different reasons, children often lose their natural curiosity and learn that it is more cool to appear disinterested, and not cool at all to be curious. Rote-learning at school and hours of daily screen watching give us ready-made input at the cost of developing our natural curiosity. Too much programmed input teaches us to be passive rather than active, and this passivity makes us more likely to be compliant consumers of cultural norms, the kind of people who will toe the party line without question.

When we are actively curious however, we develop the natural ability of the mind to think freely, and the more we exercise this mental independence, the stronger it becomes. Even if we've lost some of our natural curiosity, we can regain it. On the internet, if you search for *curiosity*, there is plenty of advice on how to enjoy the games of questioning and discovery. The main requirement is the wish to explore and some determination to follow through. If we want to develop our curiosity, it is our prerogative.

I'm going to give two examples of curiosity—both are on the subject of trying to understand intense anger. The first is, *why are the terrorists so angry?* and the second, *why are Democrats and Republicans so angry with each other?*

Why are the Terrorists So Angry?

After the 9/11 terrorist attack, there was an understandable outpouring of anger in the United States and in many other countries. Sometimes this anger was accompanied by blanket judgments about Arabs and Muslims. What if this was changed into a statement of curiosity: *I wonder why these terrorists are so angry?* Might this question lead to more understanding?

Some might object to this line of inquiry with concerns like: *Isn't this unpatriotic? Shouldn't we defend our country? Doesn't trying to understand this violence make it seem like we're OK with it, or that we should feel sorry for the perpetrators?*

By seeking to understand the reasons for violence, I am not suggesting that we ignore acts of violence against our country or condone such actions. On the contrary, a better understanding of cause may lead to better future policies for this country and for the world. And greater understanding may change our own violent, reactive thoughts, which are unpleasant to experience and not so conducive to effective solutions.

When I did research into why the terrorists are so angry, I came across a book called *Destiny Disrupted: A History of the World Through Islamic Eyes*, written by Tamim Ansary, an American citizen with Arab and Muslim roots. I was interested to take a look at world history from his perspective. Ansary writes in an informative and detached style and is not shy about detailing politics and atrocities by Muslims, Christians, and secular governments alike. After reading about centuries of Western (mostly European) domination over Arab countries, I was struck by one recent historic event. Ansary writes, matter-of-factly, about how in 1953 the U.S. Central Intelligence Agency organized a coup in Iran, and then comments:

> It would be hard to overstate the feeling of betrayal this coup embedded in Iran or the shudder of anger it sent through the Muslim world.

I decided to get the Western viewpoint on this coup and read the CIA official records that are now in the public domain. Here is how the CIA described U.S. responsibility in the coup:

> The military coup that overthrew Mosaddeq and his National Front cabinet was carried out under CIA direction as an act of US foreign policy, conceived and approved at the highest level of government.

Highest level of government? That would be President Eisenhower. It turns out that both the U.S.A. and the U.K. were jointly involved in a plan to change the democratic government of Iran into a dictatorship. Yet in previous years both countries had publicly stated their support of democracy all over the world. So, what was going on? I was particularly interested in this since I was born in England and have lived in the U.S. for the past twenty-five years.

I found that in 1953, the U.S. and Britain were, indeed, both responsible for this coup — through the secret services of CIA and MI6 respectively — against Iran's elected prime minister, Mosaddeq (who, before the coup, had been largely pro-American). Mosaddeq did not agree to the British Anglo-Iranian Oil Company's sharing of oil profits — 85 percent for Britain's AIOC and 15 percent for Iran. When the AIOC would not budge, Mosaddeq canceled the lease with the AIOC and said he would nationalize Iranian oil.

The British foreign secretary, Sir Anthony Eden, was powerless to do anything without U.S. help. Under President Truman, the U.S. had declined to interfere, but the Eisenhower administration was, according to the *Guardian*, "easily persuaded" by a claim from the British government, not supported by credible evidence, that Iran was in danger of becoming communist. While the British (through MI6) instigated the idea of the coup, the U.S. (through the CIA) implemented it. Mosaddeq was imprisoned, and absolute rule was handed over, as pre-arranged, to Mohammad Reza Pahlavi, who had signed a treaty with the U.S., giving an international consortium of oil corporations the task of managing Iran's oil. Pahlavi became the shah (king) of Iran for the next twenty-six years. Once in power, the CIA helped train SAVAK, the Shah's brutal secret police.

Hundreds of Iranians were killed in this coup. The anger of the people of Iran, and of millions of Muslims in other Middle Eastern countries, is easy to envisage: imagine how we Americans would feel if foreign powers imprisoned our president and put their chosen dictator in power over the U.S. so that they could extract oil from Texas on terms highly favorable

to them. Imagine our reaction to our democracy being annihilated by a foreign country (a country that,
at the same time, publicly proclaimed its support for
democracies worldwide). And then multiply this by
twenty-six years of rule by an unelected despotic king
whose brutal secret police were trained and supported
by this foreign power. How would we feel?

The result of this action by America and Britain
is that Muslims in general, and the Iranians in particular, could no longer trust America. (They had lost
trust in Britain long before this.) We—the U.S.—had
put monetary gain above our own stated principles of
support for democracy and respect for the sovereignty
of other nations.

According to the *Guardian* newspaper, U.S. officials have expressed regret about the coup though have
not issued an official apology. The CIA still claims its
actions were based on concern about the spread of
communism. The British government has never officially acknowledged its role.

The repercussions of distrust and fury with the
U.S. still reverberate today. Between Iran and the U.S.,
there has been an angry game of tit-for-tat ever since.
When Iranian students took U.S. diplomats and citizens hostage in 1979, the students demanded an apology for the 1953 coup, which the U.S. did not give.
The American public was incensed about the impris-

onment of these hostages and genuinely did not know the history that had preceded it. We could not have known, for example, that while the death toll among the U.S. hostages was zero, the death toll from our own government's organized coup in Iran was in the hundreds.

The repercussions were not limited to Iran. The anger about this foreign intrusion reverberated throughout the Muslim world. It is this kind of anger—the Iran coup is one example of many—that eventually fueled Al Qaeda and Isis with ready volunteers from different countries willing to die for their cause. The 9/11 terrorists came from four different Muslim countries, none from Iran, and more than 75 per cent from Saudi Arabia.

So, *why are the terrorists so angry?* The 1953 Iranian coup is just one line of inquiry. It's neither necessary nor realistic to know every reason, but even knowing just one reason begins to change the tone of a self-righteous narrative. Such understanding, as I mentioned, doesn't condone the violent actions of terrorists—any more than it condones the 1953 violence incited by the CIA with MI6 help—but it certainly can help change our own angry reaction. And yes, such understanding could create better policies going forward.

Why are Democrats and Republicans So Angry?
We can use the same process of curiosity to help understand the angry words and actions of politicians and their followers. *Why are they so upset/angry?* Or *What are they afraid of?* These can be helpful questions if they are asked with curiosity (as in *I wonder why...*) and without blame (as in *why are they so stupid?*) I looked at sociological research on reasons why people voted one way or another in the US elections. I also asked people I knew what they felt angry or fearful about, regarding matters they hoped their party would address, or regarding the opposing party. Here are a few answers, pooled from this personal and sociological research, and greatly abbreviated.

Examples from those who voted Republican:

- I'm angry that my financial situation hasn't improved for a long, long time. Decades. My family and I used to vote Democrat, but those Democrats changed. They started caring about their big-money donors and stopped caring about people like us with less income. I'm angry with the Democrats for abandoning us.

- I'm angry with the whole damn political system. I'd like to see the whole thing pulled down. That's why I voted for Donald Trump who was different, who would disrupt things.

We need a big change.

- I'm upset about abortion. I believe that a baby has a soul at conception and that it is morally wrong to have an abortion.

- I'm afraid of being controlled by socialists and big government. I want to make my own decisions and not be bogged down in bureaucracy.

- I don't want higher taxes that would be levied by Democrats.

- I'm afraid of losing my job, and my sense of usefulness, as jobs move to lower-paid workers in China or to immigrants here.

Examples from those who voted Democratic:

- I'm angry that the 1 percent continue to get richer and that the 99 percent continue to get poorer. I'm angry that the Republicans reduce taxes on the rich but don't improve the lot of the 99 percent.

- I'm angry that women are paid less than men for the same job.

- I'm angry that Republicans try to control women by taking away support for contraception and by denying a woman's rights to control her own body, including the right to choose abortion when it is needed.

- I'm upset about the environment, that we are making the world a worse place for our children and grandchildren, and that the Republicans are ignoring independent science and selectively listening to deliberately falsified science, financed by polluting industries that are major Republican donors.

- I'm afraid of our checks and balances being overturned as the White House becomes increasingly powerful and disdainful of Congress.

- I'm afraid that we are moving toward a fascist state.

You may argue with any of these statements. They may not seem logical or real to you, especially if they come from the other party, but they *are* some examples of what people feel. And that matters, because people act on what they feel. Seeing so many different reasons — and there are surely more — may help us abandon the one giant dehumanizing box into which we may be tempted to stuff all opposition voters: *They are a bunch of racists... They are lily-livered pacifists, living on handouts...* When the box is gone, we see human beings with pain and needs and wishes and dreams.

Of course, it's also true that these lists of peeves and concerns have been manipulated by political parties. The party apparatus teaches people these positions. Each side tries to enroll potential followers into angry blame of the other side, or fear of what the other side might catastrophically do.

It is not easy to remain free of the group pressure of one's political party. It may be tempting to blame those who are manipulated, thinking of them as fools, and this might add to our outrage—as in *how could they get sucked in by that lie?* But if we exchange judgment for curiosity, we may find some understanding, and we'll probably feel a whole lot better.

Over the last twenty years, I've often wondered why whole populations are so easily persuaded into believing things that are not true—no matter what their level of intelligence. And I've been curious about why anger is so effective at enrolling people into blame? What is it about anger that is binding and blinding?

Anger is so contagious that everyone hearing a speaker's anger about the other group—especially if they have rapport with that speaker—may *feel* the danger of the other group. Because the feeling is real, it seems that the danger must also be real. And, therefore, the anger seems fully justified. *It must be true; I can feel it.*

In this way, anger can be very effective at cohering one group into action against another group—but anger is not so great on discernment. Anger looks for an enemy to blame and does not see too well the real cause of its discomfort, just as a swarm of aggravated hornets will sting anything in sight.

When anger is set alight, the fire equally consumes a piece of old wood and a Steinway grand piano. Anger disconnects the neurons in our rational forebrains—when anger predominates, we tend to lose our reasoning and it is not always easy to know why we are angry. But once we are angry, our anger spreads from person to person, binding whole populations in anger-agreements on the terribleness of others.

The others, of course, are deeply offended by the accusations and retaliate by being equally or more offensive back, and so it spirals upward—upward in heat but not in kindness.

In searching for reasons, we may or may not agree with what we find about others' beliefs. But either way, the search puts us in a calmer frame of mind. Our search to find the personal, human reasons for why someone makes a decision we don't agree with can change our judgmental stance. Once the *them* become people with lives and concerns like our own, we no longer see them as the enemy. Then the pain of our own aversive emotional reaction can be transmuted to the more pleasant realms of peacefulness, relaxation, understanding, and empathy.

And then we can talk to each other again.

All we need to do is keep asking ourselves, with kindness and a little wonder: *Why?...Yeah, but why?*

Curiosity aces otherizing.

CHAPTER 11

The Relief of Seeing the Bigger Picture

You may feel a number of upsetting emotions when you disagree with or dislike an elected president, prime minister, or other official, or when the party you oppose is voted into power. You may feel anger or disappointment that your preferred outcome has not come about. Over time, it helps, a little, to see the broader picture. How, for example, a two-party system tends to alternate, and how public opinion swings, like a pendulum, back and forth. It also helps to see that over longer periods (say fifty to a hundred years), despite the four-year, eight-year, or even sixteen-year swings of opinion, there are some positive movements in terms of greater freedoms for more people. For example, women can vote.

Following the first National Women's Rights

Convention in the U.S. in 1859, it took seventy years of determined fighting by many courageous women for women's enfranchisement to come about, but it appears to be a lasting freedom. Seeing a longer time-period for change is not to encourage complacency, but to avert a reaction of fear, anger, or despondency.

Nevertheless, when I see people in power doing things I consider unethical, sometimes I lie awake, angry. I'm unable to get back to sleep because I'm busy asking, *how can they sleep at night?*

As if in answer to this question, I ran across a 1961 book I'd been given some twenty years ago: *The New World of Philosophy*, written by Abraham Kaplan, who was then professor of philosophy at UCLA. The book had not been opened for many years and smelled, not unpleasantly, of old paper. I had no intention of reading the book, but absent-mindedly opened it, scanned a few paragraphs, and... was astonished. I had happened onto an understanding of ethics and morality that I'd never come across before. The chapter described a 2,500-year-old Chinese classification of various levels of morality based on the wisdom of Confucius and Lao Tse. And, amazingly, this provided an answer to my question, *how can they sleep at night?* (And how can I?)

Levels of Moral Attainment

According to Kaplan's summary of ancient Chinese philosophy on morality, there are five fundamental levels of moral attainment—three of which are pertinent to the question of morality in politics.

Level 1—No ethics within

At this most basic level, a person has no inner sense of morality. He conforms only to the morality that is imposed by others. He does whatever he can get away with. He might avoid doing something where there is a danger of unpleasant social sanctions (e.g., imprisonment, death). In this category are psychopaths, sociopaths, and the kind of business or political leaders who damage others if they feel it benefits them to do so. It is to deal with this lowest level of morality that the most basic laws are required.

Level 2—The morality of duty

At this level, some ethical awareness has been internalized in the mind but not in the heart. Emotional impulses are more or less contained by a wall of moral obligation. Thought and feeling may, therefore, be contrary, since duty may conflict with personal desire.

Level 3—The morality of human-heartedness

At this higher level, morality is based not on duty but, primarily, on empathy for others. This is the level of the Confucian Golden Rule—*Do unto others as you would have them do unto you*—choosing to behave with consideration, not because it's your duty but because of your compassionate understanding. Here, there need be no conflict between personal wishes and duty because your empathy connects you to others. You *want* to be helpful because of this compassionate connection.

The fourth and fifth levels involve the recognition and experience of oneness in all people. Mahatma Gandhi could be an example of level 4. If you are interested in these higher levels, please see the notes at the end of the book.

I think that a significant number of people who choose to go into politics are at levels 1 and 2. People at level 1 are often highly motivated to find means of gaining power, and politics may be one of these means. Level 1 people tend to do anything they can get away with in order to increase their power. Commonly, they experience positive feelings toward those who agree with them and anger with those who don't. The conditional positive feeling may be labeled "compassion" or "caring" by the level 1 person, but it is actually a form of manipulation. The proof of this is that the positive regard disappears the moment there is disagreement. True compassion is unconditional. Level 1 people can sleep well at night because they believe that what they do is right, no matter what pain it causes others.

Level 2 politicians are more likely to follow the rules, but without heartfelt caring for those in the country they serve. Since political rules have so many loopholes, they have no problem using these loopholes to win political battles, even if their legal winning is inhumane, unethical, or causes suffering. They can sleep well at night because, in their minds, they have done their duty in following the rule book.

Those at either level 1 or 2 are unlikely to move to a higher level of morality because their primary interest is success within the bounds they perceive—either the framework of what needs to be done to win or the frame of what is allowed by duty. Such people, therefore, rarely seek self-examination or change.

I found that seeing all this was actually a relief: it was easier to accept someone's limitations than wage a battle in my own mind about how they *ought to be different*. Accepting someone's limitations does not mean we do not fight for better outcomes; it means we can fight more effectively with less anger, and with more knowledge of what we are dealing with.

Politicians at level 3 (probably rarer) are more likely to act as true servants of the people. Level 1 and 2 politicians tend to dub level 3 politicians as *weak, unrealistic* or, in the U.S., *unAmerican*.

The Sweep of History

Whatever is happening now has very likely happened before, and probably many times, over the centuries. Patterns repeat themselves over millennia. Those in power tend to do the same things they have always done, and remembering this perspective is helpful. Throughout history, in most forms of government (e.g., chiefdoms, kingdoms, feudal societies, communist regimes, fascist regimes, capitalist countries), those at the top often accumulate tremendous power and riches at the expense of the majority.

In just the last hundred years:

- Fascist dictators have maintained absolute power. Their will was what came to pass in the lands they ruled. Those who were caught disobeying died.

- Communist regimes used a convenient Marxist phrase, *the dictatorship of the proletariat,* to excuse the absolute dictatorship of the ruler who, effectively, owned every piece of land in the country. Those who were caught disobeying died.

- Capitalist democracies, to varying but often significant degrees, have allowed the very rich (the 0.1 percent) to determine policies of government that increase the wealth of the already wealthy. Those who fought inequity did not usually die, but the rich got richer and the poor got poorer. In the U.S., 40 percent of the wealth is owned by 1 percent of the people.

What those in power can and cannot get away with has varying limits, depending on the times, the culture, and the system of government.

In the 20th century, Stalin, Mao, and Hitler were, between them, responsible for the deaths of around 70 million people — many millions exterminated because they were, or were thought to be, a challenge to the ruler. In elections in democratic countries, some politicians will also do anything to win, though their choices are usually more limited by social regulations. In well-established democracies, politicians cannot, for example, get away with killing people, but character assassinations are OK. These politicians can't close down newspapers and TV stations, but they can rail against critical media or promise big perks to the media moguls who support them. They can't exterminate the educated classes, but they can remove funding for education and belittle intelligent analysis and scientific findings.

In short, they cannot control the media, their opposition, and education as drastically as absolute dictators, but they can still exert considerable influence.

FREEDOMS THAT CAN BE CONTROLLED	ACTIONS TAKEN BY DICTATORS	ACTIONS TAKEN BY WIN-AT-ANY-COST POLITICIANS IN DEMOCRACIES
Media	Imprison or kill critical journalists.	Castigate critical journalists.
	Ban media not in support of the dictator.	Demean media that report unfavorably.
	Create state media that support the actions of the dictator.	Make alliances with media corporations that support the actions of the politician.
Opposition	Assassinate or imprison opponents.	Assassinate characters; threaten imprisonment.
Education	Kill the educated classes to prevent educated rebellion.	Reduce funding for education.

The Limits of Democracy

Democracy has limits, and it's helpful to see these for what they are. Winston Churchill famously commented, "Democracy is the worst form of government, except for all those other forms that have been tried from time to time." In the first century of its existence, the U.S. government did not allow women, Native Americans, or those designated as slaves—that is, more than half the adult population—to vote. Yet even this was an improvement over the democracy in ancient Greece, the first known democracy, where the only voters were upper-class males. Most modern democracies, including the U.S., still have their quirks and limitations.

Consider, for example, these seven factors that affect democratic participation in the U.S.

1. The make-up of the U.S. Senate only partially reflects the will of the country's voters. Because the Senate, as stipulated by the U.S. Constitution, is made up of 2 senators per state, and different states vary considerably in population, the Senate does not represent the population proportionally. More than half of the senators represent 18 percent of the U.S. population while the remaining senators — fewer than half — represent the remaining 82 percent of the population.

2. The election of the U.S. president is determined by the Electoral College and not the total number of votes cast for the competing candidates. This sometimes results in a president being elected without holding the majority of votes nationwide.

3. Supreme Court justices, Court of Appeals judges, and District Court judges are nominated

by the president and confirmed by the Senate (which is elected with disproportionate representation). This means that a Supreme Court justice — a position of enormous consequence that continues for the life of the justice — can be confirmed by a body (more than 50 percent of the Senate) that is elected by only 18 percent of the U.S. population.

4. Some of the least wealthy citizens are effectively disenfranchised by certain state laws that require proof of identity that some poorer people do not have or cannot afford.

5. Those who have been in prison — even, sometimes, for minor offenses or for offenses no longer considered to be crimes — are banned from voting in most states for the rest of their lives.

6. Gerrymandering also disenfranchises voters. There are currently no laws against creating artificial political boundaries to give a political party with fewer votes more seats in government.

7. Some large corporations, run by the richest 0.1 percent, have a disproportionate influence on government policy.

You may not agree with every item on this list, or you may feel that there are mitigating circumstances with some of them. Most politicians deny, condone, or lament these limitations depending on the advantages or disadvantages they give to their party. When you read the whole list, however, it is difficult not to accept that there is some room for improvement in our democracy.

Many democracies, perhaps all, have differing sets of limitations. There is, however, one limitation that is a problem in democracies all over the world — the last-but-definitely-not-least point above: the disproportionate influence of some large corporations. The battle to limit undue corporate power in politics has been waged by some governments, with mixed success, ever since modern democracies began.

Large corporations may finance the election campaigns of most politicians who are expected, by unwritten agreement, to protect the interests of the corporation above the interests of their constituents. Politicians who do not meet this expectation will not receive the same financial backing in the future and may not get re-elected.

Big corporations have immense lobbying power. For example, in the U.S., corporations in the finance sector have three-thousand full-time, paid lobbyists, five for each member of Congress, and these lobbyists pressure the government to create favorable breaks for the finance industry, even if this reduces the earnings or investments of the majority of the country's citizens—which is what happened, catastrophically for some, in the 2008 financial crisis.

Leaders of large corporations are often given high government office, and vice versa—the well-known "revolving door" between politics and business. Former corporate leaders may use their new governmental power to create policies that improve their business more than the common good. Most of the government leaders and advisors who created the policies that caused the 2008 economic collapse were formerly leaders in major banks. Many returned to bank positions after their stint in government. It had been in their financial interest to create legislation that favored top executives in banks, even though it was not in the financial interest of the country or of 99.9 percent of its people.

Media corporations may have a particularly strong influence on elections, since they have control over the broad content put out by the media they own. They, therefore, have power to sway millions of voters and to direct their audience to make choices for politicians who protect the media-owner's corporate success. I mention in chapter 5 the research that estimated that one media mogul, Rupert Murdoch—by telling his editors to write the opposite of what they believed—created more than half a million votes for Tony Blair, the politician whom Murdoch wanted to become prime minister of the UK. If one man effectively has more than 500,000 votes, how is that democracy?

Seeing a realistic picture of some of the limits of democracy, or at least democracy as we now know it, may seem a bit daunting. But it can be useful in diminishing our outrage about particular events that we feel are unfair but which are allowed by current laws. This, of course, does not mean that we should not try everything in our power to improve our democracy over time.

The Future

In looking over this chapter, I have to admit that seeing the big picture is not a cure-all for our discontent with the powers that be. But it can help. The fraught, adrenaline-laden *OMG! How could they do that!* turns into a calmer *here we go again; what can we do to change this?* Dropping the frenzy feels a lot better. And it does not diminish our drive to fight for making a difference; in fact, usually it makes us more effective.

If you are feeling upset about the morality of some politicians and the legally-instituted limits of our democracy, there is something you can do that can make a difference to your state of mind and to your effectiveness in creating change. It involves focusing your energy on the future that you wish for. This is not a matter of some pie-in-the-sky placebo. William Blake wrote: "What is now proved was once only imagined." Imagination really does drive change—this has been true of pretty well every human advancement. The 19th Amendment in 1919 gave American women the power to vote, but this was preceded by an unknown number of women, over an unknown number of decades, imagining that this day would be possible and then acting on that imagination.

When we think of the limitations of what is happening now, our emotions tend to become adrenalized into *oh no!*—anger with the present and fear of the future. Unpleasant. Sometimes paralyzing. But when we imagine the ideal, we are bathed in the elevated feelings of contentment, peacefulness, calm, compassion, kindness and courage. These elevated feelings do not only feel good, they actually encourage creativity and resourcefulness.

You can practice focusing on the future in the following exercise.

EXERCISE

Time Travel

In this exercise you will need to close your eyes throughout most of the steps — which will make it difficult to read them. I recommend audio if it is possible for you. You can either record steps 2 to10 yourself and then listen to that recording, or, you are welcome to use my audio instructions, which you can find free of charge by signing in to my website at:

doctorgillett.com/free-freakin-exercises

Once again, make sure you have alone time in a space you feel comfortable in. Or, you can do this exercise with a friend or friends. If not required for emergency response, turn off all phones and other possible sources of electronic interruption. Sit in a comfortable chair, and have a pen and a journal, notebook, or paper to write on.

The exercise takes around ten minutes. Here is the written version.

1. Allow yourself to dream of a change in society or politics that you would like to see happen in the future. Write it down.
2. Close your eyes.
3. Take a few deep breaths and relax your body.
4. Imagine that you are sitting in a time machine.

You see in front of you a green button marked *START* and a large dial marked with every year from 2020 to 2100. You set this dial to the year 2050. In a moment you are going to travel to the year 2050. Even though everything around you will age as you move into the future, you yourself will not age at all.

5. You press the *start* button. You hear a swooshing sound. Within a few seconds you have been catapulted into the future. The year is 2050.

6. You get out of the time machine.

7. It is 2050. You see the change you wrote down earlier, in reality, before you. This change has already come about. How do you experience this change? What exactly do you see? What do you hear? Notice how you feel when you see these positive changes in the reality around you. How does your body feel? What emotions arise?

8. And now, still in the year 2050, you look back to see some of the steps that were taken to reach this change. What key event or events happened that led to this change taking place? What was a key step that led to the reality you are now in?

9. And now, still in the year 2050, but looking back a little further: what did you do that contributed, even the tiniest amount, to this new reality?

10. And now set your time machine back to the present day. It is [today's date].

11. Open your eyes and write down what happened for you. Include:

- The positive changes that you saw in 2050.

- The feelings you experienced when you saw the positive changes in the reality around you in 2050.

- The event(s) that led to those changes.

- The actions you took that contributed, even the smallest amount, to the future reality you envisaged.

If you would like to go on and make your imagined contribution to your dream actionable, you can use the exercise in chapter 9: "Clarifying Power and Action."

CHAPTER 12

Beyond All Prejudice

I was riding on the subway in New York City, recently, and saw a morose looking guy sitting opposite me. I was busy making all kinds of assumptions and judgments about this man, even his political affiliation, when I suddenly thought: *Hey, wait a minute! What am I doing? I know nothing about this guy or what kind of life he has.* So, then I changed my focus and began to think about all the things we have in common. I chose some pretty universal human values like cherishing self-respect and appreciating kindness. And here's the amazing thing: in less than a minute, I felt happier! I smiled a little in reaction to my happier feeling, and then this man smiled a little too.

It struck me that we are, each of us, faced with this kind of choice many times each day: shall I focus my mind on differences between myself (or my group) and others, or shall I focus my mind on what we have in common? Which one of these two choices we make may have a big effect on our level of happiness.

When we focus on differences—whether these are of race, hairstyle, dress, political party, sexual identity, country, class, education, wealth—judgment and prejudice easily follow. In this chapter, I'm focusing more on racial and political prejudices. There is a common means of overcoming these prejudices, and indeed all prejudice, as you will see at the end of this chapter.

"Comparison," President Theodore Roosevelt once said, "is the thief of joy." When we are focused on differences, we tend to compare ways in which we are better than—or sometimes worse than, but more often better than—the other. This is a slippery slope. As soon as we make this kind of judgment—*better than, worse than*—we have become divisive. We have divided ourselves from the other. We have slipped, often imperceptibly, into the realm of prejudice. We have turned the other into one who is *different*, who is not quite *one of us*. We perceive this person as somewhat alien. As this process of differentiation goes on, it's a short road from *alien* to *enemy*. And then, automatically and unconsciously, we find we have to protect ourselves against the enemy we have created in our minds. This makes us tense, and tension does not feel pleasant at all. Pleasure and prejudice are inversely proportional.

When we focus on commonality, by contrast, we automatically relax. There is no enemy to defend against, therefore no need to be tense. We can still disagree on a subject while recognizing and experiencing our common humanity — remembering, for example, that we share all the same basic human attributes, like caring about family, wishing to be appreciated, loving to laugh, enjoying good food, and wanting to be heard.

Racial Prejudice

A black person and a white person are genetically somewhere between 99.9 and 99.99 percent identical. The genes involved with external differences in appearance, by which we divide races, amount to just one ten-thousandth of all our genetic material! In the case of these minute racial differences, our choice seems pretty compelling: *shall I focus on the .01 percent of difference between us or shall I focus on the 99.99 percent of similarity?*

Caucasian prejudice against African Americans is a strange phenomenon. Not only is it mathematically bizarre to focus so much energy onto one ten-thousandth of another person, it is also strange in terms of our origins.

An African American, as anybody knows, is an

American who has family roots in Africa, even if these roots date back many generations. But the truth is, we all have family roots in Africa. No exceptions. There is overwhelming paleontological, archeological, and genetic evidence that the human race started in the heart of Africa. Sometime (or times) in the last hundred thousand years or so—a pretty short period in geological terms—modern human beings migrated from Africa to the rest of the world. Perhaps we should speak of African Europeans, African Chinese, African Indians, African Australian aboriginals, African Australian colonialists, African Russians, African Innuit, African Native Americans. Without this African origin, none of us would be here. We all come from the same place (Africa) and the same stock (Africans).

The massively complex human cerebral cortex—the most significant differentiator between human beings and other creatures—was also created and developed in Africa. Our rational intelligence is an African product.

With regard to skin color, some of us are purer African, perhaps, while others of us have become more discolored. When human beings migrated from Africa into the north of the Northern Hemisphere, it became advantageous to lose the natural pigmentation in the skin. In regions with a lot of sunlight, the skin needs pigmentation to protect the body from damage from ultra-violet light. It is our natural sun-block. But when Africans spread to northern areas where there was much less sunlight, a problem arose because of the vital need for Vitamin D, which is manufactured in the skin in response to sunlight. In lower sunlight areas, the skin must be less pigmented to let in extra sunlight for the synthesis of vitamin D. This is probably why human skin—through a series of genetic mutations—began to get lighter-colored in northern climes.

Today, we can ingest vitamin D through our choice of diet and supplementation, so the old advantage of lighter skin in lower sunlight areas is no longer so relevant. Today dark skin carries the original advantage of protection against ultra-violet light—which is why dark-skinned people age less visibly and are less prone to skin cancer—whereas light skin carries no known physical advantages.

So why then—if prejudice based on skin color is so strangely irrational—does it occur at all? Here are three reasons that make some kinds of prejudiced thinking (but that does *not* mean prejudiced action) inevitable in pretty much everyone:

1. *Our sense organs are primed to notice contrasts*

We tend to notice whatever is different from what we are used to. If there is one red sheep in a field of a hundred white sheep, which will you look at? We have an ancient protective mechanism that is geared to seek out differences. Walking in the wild, we see hundreds of plants, yet we notice the one plant in which the branches are moving—perhaps there is danger lurking in there? The more afraid we are, the more hyper-alert we become to the slightest difference, to anything that is out of the ordinary. As soon as we fear something that is different, we tend to otherize it.

Fortunately, we human beings also inherit enormous brain capacity, which gives us the power to observe our own reactions and make different choices.

2. We tend to otherize those who are different

Observations of mice and chimpanzees show that these animals are kinder to those considered to be kin. Chimpanzees, for example, may be very considerate of their own group but vicious to other groups; they may attack members of alien clans, sometimes even killing them. Experiments on mice have shown that they too have tribal empathy, demonstrating empathy for cage-mates in pain but not for strangers in pain.

In the same way, we human beings can be kind to those we think of as our own but unkind and uncaring to those we deem to be different. Most of us have some empathy for people we consider to be our kin. When, however, we otherize those we consider different, we switch off our capacity for compassion. When we make a group *other*, the enemy so created by our minds invokes our fight/flight, anger/fear response. It is actually impossible to experience the anger/fear response and compassion at the same time. Anger/fear is an aversive response *against* the other; compassion literally means feeling *with*. *Com* = "with." *Passion* = "feeling." Anger/fear excludes; compassion includes.

Once we have this otherizing reaction, even if it is never spoken and only shows in our body language, the one we have deemed *other* tends to have an otherizing counter-reaction. Prejudice fosters counter-prejudice.

The good news is that we do not have to go this way. Yes, we have an inbuilt tendency to otherize those we consider different, but, as I've mentioned, *a biological tendency is not a biological imperative.* We have also inherited a capacity for profound empathy for anyone we choose, and we are blessed with the amazing complexity of our cerebral cortex, which offers us a vast choice in understanding and reaction.

3. We respond to the pressure of a thousand cultural cues

The tendency toward divisiveness is also supported by cultural biases. In the U.S., a dominant white culture supplies cues, mostly unconsciously, that associate *white* with *more than* and *black* with *less than*. These cues come from assumptions held by the people we meet; from books, movies, TV, the news, etc. When the author Malcolm Gladwell took a test called the Implicit Association Test (IAT) that measured unconscious bias, he experienced what he described as "a growing sense of mortification." Though he, like most of us, consciously thought of the various races as being equal, his results showed some "automatic preference for whites." Since Malcolm Gladwell has a white father and black mother, this result was especially surprising to him. Some 80 percent of those who take these unconscious bias tests in the U.S. have pro-white associations, even though the vast majority would never consider themselves even slightly racist. The test shows that our unconscious attitudes are often at variance with our stated values. It seems we just can't help imbibing some of the norms of our culture.

Recognizing our tendencies toward bias and prejudice is immensely useful. Once we admit to these tendencies, we can more easily make the choice of unprejudiced action. And unprejudiced actions reduce prejudiced thoughts and feelings.

But here there is a common problem: it's called the human ego. The ego, which doesn't like to admit to weaknesses, genuinely believes *I'm not prejudiced.* The ego usually likes to be seen as good and so cannot easily admit to favoring one group unfairly, or even to being unconsciously influenced by society's norms. This perhaps goes some distance toward explaining why so much racist action is unconscious. It might, for example, be one of the reasons why in the U.S. a black man is thirteen times more likely to be sent to prison on drug charges than a white man, even though the sentencing judges would not admit to (or probably have any recognition of) being prejudiced.

Admitting our own tendencies to discriminate differences is, therefore, enormously helpful, because then we can do something about it. On the other hand, when the ego denies prejudice because it looks bad, then it is pretty much impossible to correct—the ego has convinced us that we don't have anything *to* correct.

So, with racial prejudice, there is an initial sensory difference that can be magnified till it colors the whole canvas of our imagination. This 0.01 percent difference can then be used by the personal ego *(I'm better than him/her)* or by the collective or tribal ego *(we are better than they are)*. Pride and prejudice. Ongoing prejudice is always based on pride in our differences, even though, as I've said, this pride can be unconscious.

Political prejudice follows a similar path, except that there is no obvious sensory difference that sparks everything off.

Political Prejudice

The perceived differences with political prejudice are initially about policies, and these differences can then be multiplied out of all proportion by emotional vehemence—*we are right (and good); they are wrong (and bad)*. Once the other side becomes perceived as the enemy, the adrenaline system takes over—anger with the enemy, fear of what the enemy will do, and dehumanization of everyone who agrees with *them*. Once both sides of the political divide are in that adrenalized state of fear or anger, neuronal connections are closed down in our rational forebrains, and then our primitive lower brains—Republican lower brains and Democratic lower brains alike—duke it out. You have only to read some of the comments made on political websites to be shaken by the degree of scathing anger and violent hatred from both sides of the political divide, each side screaming about the "f...ing morons" on the other side.

Rage may also be hidden in clever barbs of humor or the cocktail sticks of pointed innuendo, but, still, no matter how indirect, these attacks can be felt by the one who is under assault.

It's easy for any of us to get attracted to the drama of emotional conflict, and it's tempting to join in. But, as I've mentioned, the more one side attacks, the more the other side counterattacks, and so on. This process of attack and counter-attack heats up the nuanced shades of gray till they distill into two stark choices: *black/white*, *either/or*, *us/them*. There is no more understanding of the other—compassion has disappeared. It is very hard for such emotionally charged enemies to have a conversation.

In theory the solution is simple: drop the otherizing accusations, defuse the anger, and recognize the human heart of the other. But how on earth do we do this when we are in a rage with what *they* have done?

Fortunately, there are practical means of defusing the situation. We don't have to fight our own upset or fear or anger. All we need to do is to change our focus—as you will see at the end of this chapter.

A Solution to All Prejudice

I've focused on political and racial prejudice as common examples that illustrate the process of prejudicial judgment. This is not to discount the many other pain-creating prejudices we may have: religious prejudice, gender prejudice, prejudices about degree of education, prejudices against poor people, and so on. All our prejudices share the same key causes, and, to a great extent, these lead from one to the next.

1. We otherize those we consider different (even though the differences we focus on are such a tiny aspect of the total person).

2. As soon as we otherize, we produce adrenaline and cortisol in reaction to the enemy we have created.

3. Once we are in the adrenalized state of fight/flight, we can no longer feel empathy or compassion.

4. We take pride in our differences, thinking we are better (or more special) than the other.

5. We often attempt to disguise our pride because it is not socially acceptable. This disguise may be so effective that we are completely unaware of being prejudiced.

All our prejudices also share the same key solution: that is, to shift our thinking from concentration on our differences to a focus on our common ground. There are many ways of doing this.

One of the most effective—as measured in hundreds of academic studies on prejudice—is to make friends with someone in the other group. In doing this, we naturally shift our focus from being wary about the other to feeling a sense of togetherness. There has been a considerable amount of research done on the neuroscience of prejudice. When two strangers meet, especially if they do not identify with each other, one of the more primitive areas of the brain, the amygdala, lights up. The amygdala is the part of the brain that activates our fight or flight responses. Other researchers have found that the level of cortisol (one of the fight/flight hormones) increases on meeting a person whom we consider different—but that this level quickly goes down once we make human contact with this person by working together on a mutual task.

We can also re-humanize other groups through learning about them. A woman with generalized judgments against Muslims told me that she had always been clear in her mind that it was only a tiny minority of Muslims who committed acts of terror, but that she could not shift her prejudice about Muslims in general—even though she knew it to be irrational. Her prejudice shifted when she read a book I've mentioned before: *Destiny Disrupted: A History of the World through Islamic Eyes*. She also said that she gained empathy for the Arabic world after seeing the movie *Queen of the*

Desert, starring Nicole Kidman. Kidman played the role of Gertrude Bell, an English woman who traveled in the desert with the Bedouin in the early 1900s and negotiated with the British on the Bedouins' behalf. In Arabia, Bell experienced the contrast between British political duplicity and a strong valuation of loyalty practiced by the Arabs she had come to know.

TV soap operas like *One Day at a Time* provide a humorous and empathic picture of Hispanic immigrants in the U.S. *Kim's Convenience* does the same for Korean immigrants in Canada. TV, books, movies, internet searches—there are many different ways we can educate ourselves about the other just by being willing to step beyond our usual choices.

When we begin the search for the humanity in the other, there are two sources of enjoyment that help dispel the old prejudice: one is the pleasure in diversity—seeing the amazing differences in the ways in which we human beings approach life and interpret the world; the second is the pleasure in empathy, the joy in the recognition of how we all, in fundamental matters, are very much the same.

When we judge these differences, it is virtually impossible to feel empathy. But as soon as we focus on commonality, then empathy and compassion naturally follow. One of the ways you can make this switch is to take part in the following exercise.

EXERCISE

The Pleasure of Finding Common Ground

This exercise demonstrates how to shift gears from focus on differences to focus on common ground. You will need to choose a person to work with, though this person does not need to know anything about what you are doing. In other words, this exercise is completely private: it is your own exploration. The person you work with could be someone of a different race, different religion, or different political position. Or it could be someone who dresses differently from you or someone who just seems to irk you for no obvious reason. You can try it on anyone at all. There are always differences that we can choose to focus on, or not.

The exercise works in any public space in which it is safe for you to give your undivided attention — sitting in a subway and observing someone sitting opposite you would be an example. It also works at home with a family member, a friend, or even someone on TV. You can also do this exercise entirely in your imagination, focusing on and visualizing a person you know. Whomever you choose, in whatever scenario, it's best if they are sitting or standing still, so that you can see or visualize them well.

If you are working with a person who is physically present, it is possible to do this exercise with your eyes open, though a lot easier if you close your eyes when instructed. Whether you close your eyes or not, please do not attempt this exercise while driving, since you would need to use active visualization. If you'd prefer to do the exercise with audio instructions, you can find these free of charge by signing in to my website at

doctorgillett.com/free-freakin-exercises

Here is the written version of the steps.

1. Look at the person sitting or standing. If the person is physically present, don't stare of course — you can look away and then look back after a while. If you are doing this exercise entirely in your imagination, close your eyes and focus on the person's image. If you can't imagine an exact image, that's fine — simply focus on imagining that the person is present for you in some way.

2. Now, focus on how this person is different from you. Make some mental judgments about this person — you can use the ones you usually use or make some new ones. For about a minute, allow yourself to really get into this silent judging.

3. If your eyes are open, close them now. Evaluate how you feel when you make such silent judgments, using a happiness scale of one to ten, ten being happiest. Open your eyes again and write down the number. This is your *differences score on happiness.*

4. Close your eyes again. Shift your focus deliberately onto what you have in common with this other person. Remember that, genetically, you are almost

identical with every other single human being in this world. Remember that you both share the same basic human wishes, needs, and values — like, for instance, the wish for acceptance by others, the wish for affection, the need for self-respect, the need for safety and shelter. You very likely share a similar desire for trust, for warmth, for having fun, for making a contribution, for self-expression, for purpose, for independence. Choose any one or a few of these universal human values that stand out as important for you. And then imagine that these same human values are just as strong in, just as important to the person you are thinking about. If this person is physically present, open your eyes and see them anew with these human values that you share.

5. How do you feel — on the same happiness scale of one to ten — when you experience your commonality? This is your *commonality score on happiness*.

Most people who do this exercise find their commonality score on happiness to be significantly higher than their differences score. If you think about this, it's pretty amazing. The exercise, in addition to showing how prejudice can quickly be overcome, demonstrates how a simple change of mental focus can affect our level of happiness and that we actually have quite a lot of control over both our thinking and our feeling. We are all the inheritors of a massive cerebral cortex—courtesy of Africa—which has the power to choose its focus. We have the power to fix our gaze on tiny differences if we want. We also have the power, whenever we would like to do so, to change our focus onto commonality. Many people who have done this exercise are surprised at how thinking of a wish or need that they value in themselves, and then imagining this same wish or need as being equally important in the other, creates almost instant empathy and compassion.

What were your differences and commonality scores? I'm collecting preliminary research figures on this. If you'd like to take part, please submit your anonymous results by entering two numbers on my website:

doctorgillett.com/commonality-survey

Shifting from focus on differences to focus on that which we have in common is both easy to do and powerful in effect. And the more you do this, the easier it is to make the shift. The reason it is so pleasurable is based both on what you are relinquishing and what you are moving toward. You are relinquishing prejudice or judgment in which you have created an enemy in your mind, an enemy who is inevitably associated with protective tension in your body — and, therefore, with a feeling of contraction.

In moving toward commonality, you experience empathy and compassion, and these are relaxed, warm, expanded, pleasurable feelings.

Reconnecting with Family and Friends

A couple of years ago, I employed a carpenter, Al, to fix our house. On one occasion, while talking innocuously about the weather, I happened to mention something about global warming. Al raised his voice. "It doesn't f...ing exist," he said. "It's all a f...ing plot to control our freedom."

Even though I'm a passionate believer in trying to protect our children's and grandchildren's environment from the damaging excesses of some human activities, I chose not to argue with this man in this moment. Firstly, based on the fieriness of his reaction, I thought that arguing about this would go nowhere useful; and secondly, I didn't want him to get distracted from the work he was doing on my house.

A couple of weeks later, I was telling a friend — an

avid ecologist—about this short conversation. Hearing that the builder in our house denied global warming, she asked me, quite forcefully, "How could you possibly work with him?"

It so happened that I had just given Al an unsolicited letter of appreciation, and I invited her to read it. Here is an excerpt:

A big thank you for all the building work you have done over the last months. From your work, it is obvious that you care about quality—you do quality work.

And you clearly care about people too. Just yesterday, you walked across the mat on the deck and stopped to look at a corner of that mat that was turned over and could have been a trip hazard. You bent down—in the rain—to straighten the corner of the soaking wet mat, and then continued on your way. I know you never told me about this—I just happened to see your act of kindness through my study window. So many people would not even have noticed the bent corner, or if they had noticed, would have walked right past. But not you—because you care. Thank you.

You also cared about how you left the place each day. I have never ever encountered builders who left the place they work in so spotlessly clean. It felt to us that you cared for the place we lived in, and therefore we too felt cared for.

You have been scrupulously honest, and I trust you completely. It was a real pleasure to work with you. If you ever need a reference for a client, ours will be a glowing one!

"Oh, I see," my friend said, "I understand why you would want to employ someone like this. But how could it have been a pleasure to work with him? Didn't his denial of global warming bother you?"

"No," I said. "I already knew that a lot of people don't think global warming is real. I didn't focus on that. I focused on Al's goodness. The more I focused on his great qualities, the more I liked him." And this led into a conversation with my friend about the art of finding commonality with our fellow human beings.

There was something else that Al taught me.

A couple of months later, I happened to notice that Al had an old scar across his right hand. I asked him how he got it.

"That's from when I was a kid," he said. "I begged my Dad to let me have a penknife, and he finally gave me one. The first time I used it, I didn't know what I was doing, and the knife snapped shut on my fingers. The blade went down to the bone. There was blood everywhere."

"Did you get stitches?" I asked.

"No, I couldn't do that. If I'd told my father what had happened, he would have beaten me bad. I just hid it and let it heal as best I could."

"Wow! Sounds like your father was pretty tough."

"Yeah, he was a hard man, very hard." He paused, and then added, perhaps with a little pride: "So, I learned to take care of myself."

This anecdote from Al's past got me thinking: might this kind of experience have contributed an element to his fierce independence—which included a strong dislike and suspicion of even a hint of control from any outside agency, personal or governmental?

Whether it did or not, Al's story also reminded me that we never truly know why people act as they do, what has befallen them, what their life experience has been, and in what ways they may have done their best to cope with their own circumstances.

Having this in mind is useful when we navigate strong differences of opinion, political or otherwise. There are several types of situation in which our navigational abilities might be tested. The rest of this chapter is about dealing with four of these—at work, with neighbors, with friends and family, and after an argument with anyone.

At Work

With colleagues and in most professional situations, where the focus is primarily on getting the job done rather than on making personal connections, it usually works out better to avoid discussing divisive political matters.

And if someone in your workplace challenges you on political differences? Evade. Without being aggressively evasive. Perhaps let him know, with a touch of light humor (combined with definitive intent), that you don't like to mix politics with work.

You could tell her, if necessary, that one of the things you most value is the freedom of people to have differing opinions and that you respect everyone's freedom of choice, whether others agree or not. In making this kind of statement, you are moving from talking about that which divides to proffering a subject of commonality—she will probably agree in the value of freedom of choice.

Meanwhile, you can privately (and deliberately) focus on what you have in common with the other and what you like about the other. Having this frame of mind helps harmonize a working relationship.

With Neighbors

This is a true story, involving two neighbors I'll call

Patricia and Tom. Patricia voted Democrat; Tom, Republican.

Patricia, who enjoyed the natural world, went to see Tom, whom she had never met before, mostly because she wanted to see his pet turkey, who was a minor celebrity in the local area. After a very brief introduction, Tom, perhaps thinking that Patricia might be liberal in her views, said, pre-emptively and with a tone of defiance, "I'm a Republican!"

"Oh," Patricia said warmly, "it doesn't matter to me who you vote for. What I care about are people's hearts, and I can see *your* heart from the way you look after your place and the love you have for your animals..."

Tom's defiance melted. They never discussed politics, and they spoke warmly to each other, sharing their mutual love of animals.

Sometimes neighbors have a hard time with signs hammered into the lawn next door, advertising candidates for election. If it's a candidate you heartily disapprove of, what do you do? The answer, of course, is *nothing*. You already know this, but what about the mental *somethings* that might be reverberating in your mind and guts—things like annoyance or judgment? Here are five mental actions you can take:

1. Remind yourself that we all have the right to hold our views and to vote in the way we choose.

2. Remind yourself that we all have the right to proclaim our views visually on our own land.

3. If you think you know why your neighbor voted the way they did, remind yourself that you probably do not. This is especially useful if your presumed reason is a judgment like *Because they're stupid.*

7. Remind yourself that how your neighbors vote is a tiny fraction of everything they are and do, and that it is just a part of their complex histories, their wishes, their needs, their virtues, their values.

8. Remind yourself of your neighbor's good qualities. If you can't think of any, find some of the human values you have in common (as described in the last chapter).

With Family and Friends

With family and friends, you may be more likely to want to maintain or re-foster a personal connection. If there are divergent political opinions, there is a decision to be made: do you think it is better to avoid political subjects altogether? Or not?

If opinions are very hot, or very cold, and you do decide to avoid the subject of politics, the next question is how? If you studiously avoid political discussion with no acknowledgment that both sides are doing this, it can be awkward, with the unacknowledged elephants and donkeys in the room making everyone feel uncomfortable with their covert trumpeting and braying. One way out of this is to have an *agree-to-disagree* truce. For example, *Look, I know we have different political opinions, and I strongly believe in our rights to our own viewpoints. I'd like to suggest that we don't get into talking about politics. I really value your company, and I don't want political disagreement to get in the way of our good family feeling. I'd like us to be able to agree to disagree and to have no bad feelings about each other having different viewpoints. What do you think of us having a moratorium on talk about politics — at least for now?*

If, on the other hand, you do decide to talk about politics, here are six things you can do — or avoid doing — that might help prevent an all-out war:

1. Do not try to convince the other person of your point of view. Even if you are sure you are right — in fact especially if you are sure you are right — this will not end positively.

2. Start by making a heartfelt connection. Focus on the commonalities you have already prepared in your mind in advance, and be sincere in your expression.

3. Listen to the other person's point of view with curiosity rather than judgment—and if you have judgment, it's OK, just don't express it.

4. Do everything in your power to find out about the other person's needs, wishes, or values that are met by the position they support. What does it give them? What does it mean to them? Cultivate your own fascination with the answers to these questions. Be an explorer: find what is in it for them. Your genuine interest will create empathy and rapport.

5. If you truly want to build rapport, demonstrating that you hear this person's point of view is perhaps the most important thing you can do. For example: *So, it sounds like you're saying that you are really scared that rising oceans might end up destroying coastal cities sometime this century, and that you want governments to do anything they can to prevent this.* Stating the other person's point of view doesn't mean you agree or disagree; it lets them know you heard them. Another example: *What I'm getting from what you said is that you feel angry about your living standard going down over the last thirty years. Your experience has been that no governments, Democrat or Republican, have addressed this, and, so, you wanted to vote for someone who would really rock the system.*

6. Only if there is a good connection between you, should you venture to bring in your own point of view. If your prime aim is to build rapport, you may not even need to do this. Sometimes, when there is good rapport, the other side may eventually ask you a question out of the interest and curiosity that you have just modeled.

After an Argument

How can you mend broken bridges between yourself and others after you've argued heatedly—or distanced yourself coldly—over differing political affiliations? If you've had an argument with friends or family members and you are still experiencing lingering anger and you would like to make contact again—perhaps even make amends—the preparatory exercise that follows can be very helpful.

EXERCISE

Dissolve Animosity after a Disagreement

For this exercise, make sure you have alone time in a space you feel comfortable in. If not required for emergency response, turn off all phones and other possible sources of electronic interruption. Sit in a comfortable chair, and have a pen and a journal, notebook, or paper to write on.

This is another closed-eye exercise. If you would like to follow an audio version of this exercise, you can access this on my website:

doctorgillett.com/free-freakin-exercises

Here is the written version of the steps.

1. Close your eyes. Imagine you are with the person you had the disagreement with. Picture the scene from your point of view, looking at this aggravating person in front of you. For about twenty seconds, imagine yourself arguing your point of view.

2. In a moment, I'm going to ask you to allow yourself to disassociate from your own point of view. To do this, imagine that you actually jump out of your own body, so to speak. Your body remains where it was, arguing away, while your mind's eye shifts to a new point of view. This new point of view is located just behind and above the shoulder of the person you are angry with. Take this position right now. Your mind's eye is

behind and above the other person's shoulder and you can see your body arguing away. Look over his or her shoulder and observe yourself arguing. You are actually seeing yourself from their point of view. What do you look like? What's it like to see yourself from the other's point of view? Be aware of how you look and what it feels like to listen to you. You can pause the audio as you do this.

3. After you have seen and felt this other person's point of view, take this other perspective with you as you allow yourself to return, gently, to your own body within the scene.

4. Now, open your eyes. Write down what came up for you. How did you look from the other's point of view? What happened for you? How do you feel?

Once you experience what it is like to see yourself from the other person's point of view, there may come a moment when you sense a shift, perhaps a softening or an inkling of surprise at what you look like and what you project when you are angry or tense.

A man who did this exercise told me, "When I was in my own body, I thought I was absolutely right. I didn't just think it. I knew it! I could not understand how it was even possible that she did not agree with me. When I jumped out of my body and looked over her shoulder, I saw myself standing there being pretty aggressive and, from her perspective, I didn't want to listen to what this person—I mean myself—was saying. No one would have wanted to listen to a person talking like I was! I was critical, disdainful, quite arrogant. Afterward, my judgments about her seemed to have melted away. I feel quite tender toward her."

In this exercise you manipulate yourself, literally, into a 180-degree shift in your point of view.

When you deliberately position yourself to see what you look like from the other person's perspective, you are almost instantly aligning yourself with the other person. You're seeing *with* this person, rather than *at* or *against* this person. Seeing *with* someone else, sharing their point of view, is an act of empathy. And empathy dissolves discord.

The reason for writing down what happened for you, is that this helps to strengthen your shift of perspective. And it helps you to remember it later. When we're angry, it isn't easy to remember that any point of view other than our own is even possible. So, we need all the help we can get to remember that there is another way of seeing the world. By writing down the shift and the positive effect it had on you, you are helping to ingrain the pathway to putting yourself into someone else's shoes in the future.

After doing this exercise, and before meeting family or friends who have uncomfortable differences of opinion, there is another piece of internal work you can do: it is to focus your mind on the positive attributes of the other person. Think of the qualities you like in this other person.

And if you can't, for the moment, think of anything you like about them, focus on what you have in common. Remind yourself that you share the same basic human wishes, needs, and values—as in the last chapter. In this way, your focus shifts from the splintering of differing ideas to the warm heart of your mutual humanity.

CHAPTER 14

The Amazing Richness of Personal Choice

There are many things over which we have absolutely no choice. We can vote, but we cannot control who will be elected. We can give our opinion, but we cannot make someone listen, and we certainly cannot make them agree with us. If the change we want involves anyone else at all, we have no definitive control over whether that change will ever happen, since other people also have choices.

And yet, what we *do* have control over determines our happiness.

We have power over what we think, what we feel, what we say, and what we do. When we align these four arenas of our power with our full-hearted intention, we have amazing possibilities—for both happiness and effectiveness.

In this book I have mentioned two opposite trends that relate to happiness. On the one hand, divisiveness destroys contentment and sabotages happiness because, by nature, it fosters the self-protective, fight/flight emotions of fear and anger, with their many variant expressions—like resentment, irritation, indignation, dislike, contempt, frustration, exasperation, outrage, unease, worry, mistrust, alarm, foreboding, dread...

When we make heartfelt connections with others, on the other hand—even if only in our imagination—we experience a very different set of feelings related to human commonality: empathy, compassion, calmness, warmth, contentment, curiosity, wonder, inspiration, gratitude, care, love, humility, kindness, respect... These are pleasurable feelings. They are feelings that also inspire greater effectiveness in our relationships with others.

If we have the intention that, whatever goes on in this world of ours, we are going to live more in connection with others than in divisiveness, then there are a number of choices—in thoughts, feelings, words, and actions—that we can make to this end. Following is a list of some of these choices—and how they relate to previous chapters.

Choosing Our Informational Inputs

Chapter 5 was on the choice to protect yourself from the divisive influences of the media by reducing your involvement with partisan, anger-stoking printed and digital content.

Of course, our informational choices are much broader than this. Every day we choose what we feed our minds.

We choose what we read, what we watch on our phones and TV, what we hear on the radio, and what we search for on the internet. We can look at books, articles, and programs that stoke the embers of judgmental energy, or we can choose items that are more compassionate in nature. We can read that which uplifts, or that which brings us down—or that which deadens us with mediocrity.

We can choose only those books, articles, and programs that support our already formed points of view. On the internet and social media, we can find something from almost any point of view, so it's easy to select only those opinions that validate our own position. In addition, the internet almost instantly reflects back to us our beliefs through algorithms controlled by businesses that make their money from enhancing fear and outrage. These algorithms offer us corroborations of the choices we've made before, encouraging us to sink further into any rut we've already begun to dig.

But still we have a choice: with a little more effort we can deliberately search for articles that give the opposite opinion on an issue and come to our own conclusions. If we do look at other sides to an issue, we have a choice of whether to use the alternative view as yet more fuel for our position *(whoa, look how stupid they are!)* or whether to consider another view with a more open mind *(let me try to understand this from their point of view; what are they concerned about? What are their wishes or needs?)*

Choosing Whom We Spend Our Time With

In many situations, we get to determine whom we spend our time with. We can choose to spend more time with people who feel good to be around, or we can choose to spend time with people who seem to pull us down or who demand allegiance to a polarized point of view. We can choose to be with more divisive people who roil the atmosphere with subtle whips of enmity, or we can choose to be with more inclusive people who radiate a sense of warmth.

Then again, we can choose to spend time with those who appear to make things better by agreeing with our limitations and judgments, or we can spend time with those who challenge us uncomfortably but beneficially.

We have so many options.

Choosing to Focus on What We Have in Common, Rather than on Differences

You may have noticed that this is a theme throughout this book. Whomever we are with — and sometimes we *cannot* choose whom we are with — we can decide to focus on what we have in common with this person (that which unites us) or we can choose to focus on differences (that which may divide us).

This choice is an essential ingredient for our own happiness and effectiveness. When we otherize, we focus on differences, and when we focus on differences, we often otherize. This is a recipe not just for separation and alienation but also for fear and anger, which are usually so unpleasant to experience. When, on the other hand, we experience the humanity we have in common, actual differences are much less likely to create division; instead they can be enjoyed with wonder and a delight in diversity.

Choosing to Focus on the Other's Abilities Rather than Liabilities

Similarly, we can focus on what's wrong with the person we're with, or on their talents and strengths, as I mentioned briefly last chapter. In moments when we find ourselves rehearsing our judgments about a person, we can deliberately focus on his or her good qualities. This really does work. One moment we can feel the unpleasant kind of tension from the covert anger

of judgment, and the next moment, by a shift of focus, we can feel relaxed and kindly. The person we are
thinking of has not changed an iota so far as we know;
we have just made a decision to change our focus.

Choosing Curiosity and the Big Picture

You can also choose to focus on the bigger picture
(chapter 11) rather than being flung around on the
vicissitudes of each day's crises.

In a 2019 NPR interview, the author Salman
Rushdie was asked why, given the current political
climate, he was still an optimist. He replied, "History
doesn't go on tramlines." He explained that it's not inevitable that things will go from bad to worse and that,
in his experience over decades, political situations can
change very quickly and unpredictably.

To see the bigger picture, curiosity is an asset.
If we assume we know who is to blame, we can easily
close ourselves down in a prison of judgment in which
bars of prejudice constrain our joy, and rays of anger
bounce from wall to wall incinerating our kindness.
Alternatively, we can choose to hone our own natural
curiosity (chapter 10) about the amazingly complex
reasons why something has occurred. When there's
no easy enemy to blame, equanimity, kindness, and
peacefulness have more space through which to rise to
the surface of our experience.

Choosing the Words We Speak

Even if we cannot, for the time being, prevent angry or fearful otherizing thoughts from arising in our mind, we can always make the choice not to voice them. Just because we think something doesn't mean we have to say it. We have absolute power over this choice: we can keep our mouths closed, or we can open them. A closed mouth gathers no foot.

Equally, we have the choice of whether to speak words of kindness that connect people, gracious words that recognize others as equals in human spirit.

Closing our mouths—while often useful and occasionally lifesaving—is, I admit, not necessarily sufficient. We can clench our jaws and stare with heavy vibes of otherizing anger without saying a word, just as we can say sweet words edged with glinting razors of sarcasm. Nevertheless, choosing our words or silence, even if we have not yet succeeded in choosing our emotions, can be a great start. By not speaking a divisive word, even if we are feeling angry, we may be spreading less divisiveness than we otherwise would.

The Courage to Make These Choices

It may not always be easy to make the choices I've mentioned, for there may be strong—though perhaps subtle—social pressure to conform to accepted ways of speaking and acting. The expectations come from family, friends, colleagues, co-workers, neighbors, political party members—anyone who knows you in a certain way and expects you to behave in your usual manner.

Deliberately choosing your sources of information, choosing whom you spend time with, choosing commonality over otherizing, choosing abilities over liabilities, choosing curiosity over blame, and choosing your words and actions in alignment with your values—all of this may take a certain amount of courage. I'm defining *courage* as the willingness to take a step that you might fear. Breaking with a norm incurs the possibility of social reactions that most of us fear—reactions like anger and rejection. And the more we are tied down by social expectations, the more courage it takes.

Sometimes we are in situations where we cannot choose whom we spend time with, or what actions we take, without incurring complete rejection by those who are dearest to us. Communities can be intense in their pressure for conformity. But even if we feel that we had better not make a certain choice—at least not for the time being—we can always choose our thoughts and feelings.

CHAPTER 15

Choose Your Thoughts, Choose Your Feelings

We have the ability to choose both our thoughts and our feelings. I admit that this is sometimes hard to believe. We're more likely to suppose the opposite. *I can't help what I feel or what I think. Sure, I can accept what I say or do is my choice—but choosing my thoughts and feelings? No, not really. They choose me.*

That is how it often seems. I, and I imagine you too, have experienced times when the mind, seemingly on its own, rehashes scenes or memories over and over again. Some of the scenes may be full of feeling, and we don't seem to be able to stop them recurring. Sometimes it seems as if we are victims of our own thoughts and feelings.

There are times, however, when we *do* change our thoughts and feelings deliberately. If you tried that exercise on finding common ground with another (chapter 12), you would have noticed that in the space of about a minute, a deliberate change of thought (from concentration on difference to concentration on commonality) led to new feelings. We can switch the channel in our own minds—without even having to find the remote—just by thinking of something else. More on this later in the chapter.

Thoughts Change Feelings

Most of our feelings are emotional reactions to the thoughts going on in our minds. The main exception to this is our emotional response to physical danger, which usually moves faster than—and so precedes—complex thoughts. If you nearly fall off a cliff, you will probably feel fear, which is a natural and useful deterrence against falling off cliffs. We usually do not have a choice about whether or not to have this kind of emotion.

Most of our *cliffs,* however, are mental. By *mental cliffs* I mean the thoughts we hold of enmity and danger, the thoughts that cause us pain. We have more choice over these feelings because we have more choice over the thoughts that created them.

If you vividly remember a terrifying scene in a movie you went to years ago, your pulse will speed up. The mental choice to remember this scene is enough to create a whole slew of emotional and physical effects: the feelings of fear associated with this thought are accompanied by increased heart rate, increased rate of breathing, increased secretion of fight and flight hormones like cortisol and adrenaline, and increased blood-flow in the fight/flight-associated amygdala in the more primitive part of the brain.

A strong judgmental thought about a politician we dislike can do the same thing. If you want to test this out (I don't recommend it), think of the politician you most dislike, focus intently on the worst thing you think they've ever done, let your judgmental feelings arise as they will, and see what happens to your heart rate. This gives you a measure of the power you allow that politician to have over you! Sometimes we imagine that disaster will follow the election of a politician we disapprove of, and this imagining of a future dark scenario then sets off a similar adrenalized train of feelings and physical effects in our bodies—even though we cannot know what the future will eventually bring.

In personal relationships, you can reverse this effect—that is, move away from fight/flight emotions—when you shift from judgment of the person to focusing on their best qualities. This shift of the focus of your mind can simultaneously change your feelings from tense disapproval, contempt, or anger to relaxed openness, kindness, or pleasure.

We have a similar choice when looking back at past events: unhappy people tend to focus on the things that went wrong for them; happier people tend to focus on the things that went well.

Choosing Our Thoughts

It's one thing to recognize that our thoughts create most of our feelings; it's another to accept that we can actually *choose* our own thoughts.

We have probably all experienced those times when our minds seem out of control and appear to be in charge of what we think.

It is in the nature of our minds to move in almost continual thought. We have thousands of thoughts per day, and a good proportion of these are repetitive, unproductive, and not highly conducive to contentment. Our minds are built to think. Like exuberant, muddy puppies, thoughts jump up on the pressed clean clothes of our mental intentions.

It is up to us how we harness this playful energy. We cannot harness it by trying to stop it. It doesn't work to tell our minds not to think—either generally or on a particular subject. For example, if I tell you not to think of a giraffe, of course you have to think of a giraffe in order to try not to think of it. In order to change your course of thinking, the trick is to make a substitution: you can't *not-think* of a giraffe, any more than you can *not-think* of a particular politician, but you can think of something else. In such simple ways we can direct our thoughts to what we decide to focus on.

Our brains can only focus on one thing at a time, and one great perk we all have is that we get to choose what that focus is. Our selection of where we focus our attention is one of the keys to our own happiness. So, yes, we *do* have the power to choose what we think—in fact our own thoughts are one of the few things over which we really do have power.

But, wait, it's not always that easy. Sometimes there is so much emotion connected to a thought, that I just can't get it out of my mind. I suppose you could say I'm choosing to dwell on it, and maybe that's true on one level, but I don't know how to stop.

When thoughts are highly charged with emotion, changing these thoughts may sometimes require a different approach...

Feelings Energize Thoughts

While it's true that thoughts create feelings, it's also true that feelings enliven thoughts. If you are angry about an insult from someone, for example, you might suddenly find yourself remembering another insult from someone altogether different. To use a computer analogy, it's as if many peeve-filled thought documents are stored in the anger file. Click on that anger file, and all the peeves are there, ready to lend support to this new angry feeling.

Another example: when you've just had an argument with someone close to you—and it's not yet resolved—do you find yourself thinking of all the other annoying things that person has ever done, or do you find yourself thinking of their finest qualities?

Sometimes the thought we have is so bound up with feeling that it's impossible to know where *thought* and *feeling* begin and end; we could call this entity a *thought-feeling*. If I have an angry, judgmental thought about someone, where is the boundary between the judgmental thought in my mind and the anger in my body? Judgment feeds anger, and anger feeds judgment in a tangle of energy...

Yes, exactly. So, what do I do when this "thought-feeling" is so strong that I don't seem to be able to shift it with a change of focus? What do I do when I'm furious about what someone has done—actions that I believe have hurt many people—and I can't change this powerful thought-feeling? What do I do when I make a real strong effort to change the focus of my thinking, but whenever I drop my guard, the old habits of thinking and feeling just come back?

Changing the Core of a Divisive Thought-Feeling

When the predominant feeling is anger, you can change the feeling through understanding the cause of the anger within you, as I describe in chapter 7, "The Pleasure of Dropping Anger, and How to Do It." I have found this successful at times of outrage.

In addition, or alternatively, you can do the following exercise which is a kind and effective way of opening a slammed door of judgment:

EXERCISE

The Four Questions

One of the best methods I've encountered for changing thought-feelings that seem too strong for us to shift is a form of self-inquiry taught by the author Byron Katie. Katie, who in the 1980s had suffered from depression, phobia, and addiction, describes an epiphany in 1986 when she stopped believing that her negative thoughts were reality. Since then Katie has taught millions four questions that create freedom from fixed positions of judgment. Her method has been recommended by many professional therapists, including the bestselling author Dr. Daniel G. Amen, psychiatrist, clinical neuroscientist and brain-imaging expert. Here are Katie's four questions:

1. Is it true?

2. Can you absolutely know that it's true?

3. How do you react — what happens — when you believe that thought?

4. Who would you be without that thought?

Following, in the next few pages of this book, is why I think these questions can be so effective, especially when we have emotionally-charged, judgmental thoughts.

Question 1. Is it true?

Question 2. Can you absolutely know that it's true?

The power of these two questions can be quite surprising. There is no direct challenge. No one is saying, *Hey, what you think is not true,* which would incur defensiveness. They're just questions, sparks for the gentle fire of self-inquiry. If we ask these questions to ourselves, with a genuine interest in finding the truth, it is usually very difficult to say yes to both of them. The answer to the second question is, nearly always, *no,* because we realize that we cannot be absolutely sure that our judgmental thoughts about something are the whole truth. There must surely be things we don't know, especially if it's about a person we've never met, and—almost certainly—about anyone at all.

Let's take two popular political beliefs, each believed by tens of millions of people: *Hillary Clinton is a criminal* and *Donald Trump is stupid*. Each of these beliefs is associated with feelings of anger, disgust, contempt, and/or hatred.

Question 2: *Can I absolutely know that it's true? Can I be completely certain that Hilary Clinton is a criminal?* No. For many reasons. On one practical level, using private email accounts for government business was not unique to Clinton: Colin Powell, John Kerry, and, more recently, Ivanka Trump, have all sent and/or received official emails through private email accounts—though on a much smaller scale. Clinton admitted she made a mistake. Did she have criminal intent? Republicans say yes. Democrats say no. The FBI, led by a Republican, concluded that criminal intent could not be proved. Given the fact that I know that politicians make up some things and exaggerate others, how can I trust what either side says about this? Politicians and media can (and did) make hundreds of different arguments about these servers, but I cannot, if I'm honest, absolutely *know* that Hilary Clinton is a criminal.

Question 2: *Can I absolutely know that it's true? Can I be completely certain that Donald Trump is stupid?* No, I cannot. He won the presidency through very clever use of social media. The analytics firm mediaQuant estimated that between October 2015 and November 2016, Trump earned the equivalent of $5.6 billion in free media reporting through his deliberate use of outrageous statements. This was a very useful advertising advantage in the lead-up to the election. Trump also understood the anger and worry of millions of people and became the mouthpiece that represented their anger. I may or may not like such tactics, but *stupid* they were not. I may think that Trump made other errors, but I cannot, truthfully, *know* that Donald Trump is stupid.

In these two examples, I attempted to give a few logical reasons why I could not *know* they were the truth. But it is not necessary to find reasons. All that is necessary is the recognition that we cannot absolutely know we are right.

One of the reasons Katie's two questions are so powerful is that they rock the black-and-white depictions of divisiveness—*I believe this and I'm right; they believe that and they're wrong.* These first two of Katie's questions challenge the absolutes, because in most cases we have to admit: *No, I cannot be absolutely sure.* The certainty is blurred, and the sharp line created by the knife-knowledge of rightness is diffused to include more possibilities: there could be a seed of doubt, some *maybes* meandering uncertainly, and perhaps a little more kindness to those who believe differently. This rocking of certainty creates an important opening: *Hey, wait a minute, my belief is not necessarily reality—this is just a thought.* Already, we have begun to de-weld ourselves from the harsh absolute of believing *My thought is the absolute reality for me and everyone else.* With this, polarization and anger diminish. The fire of blame is watered with an ounce of humility.

Question 3. How do you react—what happens—when you believe that thought?

Most people respond by saying that when they think a divisive thought, they feel tense, uncomfortable, angry, apprehensive. Believing *Clinton is a criminal,* for example, or *Trump is stupid* is often associated with hateful feelings that feel no more pleasant for the thinker than for the person being thought about. This question of self-inquiry can help clarify the emotion that surrounds the belief/thought.

Katie does not ask people to drop their belief. That would not be respectful. And it would also be counterproductive because no one likes to be told what to think or not think. The person is helped to be aware of a simple correlation: divisive beliefs—which have already been examined and found to be just thoughts, not necessarily true, and certainly not the whole truth—do not feel good to hold! It is the person's choice what he/she does with that information and whether he/she wishes to continue these beliefs/ thought processes or not.

Question 4. *Who would you be without that thought?*

Most people realize that they would actually be just fine without the divisive belief. They describe feeling more relaxed, content, and even happy while contemplating the process of dropping their judgmental belief. The question is a gentle challenge to the temptation to hold on to a divisive belief by identifying it as part of who we are. The welding of the belief to our sense of self, or ego, can be dropped without danger to ourselves. For example, if the description *Clinton is a criminal* or *Trump is stupid* is taken to be the party position and I am identified with that party position, I need to know that I'll be OK with myself if this identity is changed. I need to know it's safe.

One more step: Turn the thought around.

There is one final step that helps de-weld an emotional judgment from what we might think of as *the truth*. Katie calls it the turnaround. It's an invitation to try out the opposite of your judgment. Here are a few examples, playing with the beliefs *Clinton is a criminal; Trump is stupid*

The turnaround: *Clinton has integrity; Trump*

is smart. Or *I am a criminal; I am stupid.* These turn-arounds are ways of playing with our former absolute beliefs in order to counteract *black/white, either/or* thinking—the kind of thinking that is associated with judgment, anger, and hatred. The turnaround jangles the fixed wires of certainty.

It takes some flexibility to play this game. The reward is greater freedom from judgmental thinking. I call it a game because it should be played with curiosity, fun, and kindness to yourself. When you do the turnaround, you are not creating another absolute, nor are you putting yourself down; you are playing with another possibility. It's not *I am a criminal* as a judgment; it's more of a gentle questioning, as in: *What part of my thinking might be criminal? Could it be considered criminal—as in* my bad—*to make an absolute judgment about someone and shout "lock her up" without knowing her intention or truly understanding Clinton's alleged crime? What part of* my *thoughts might be stupid? Could it be my black-and-white thinking that refused to recognize Trump's cleverness in various arenas? Or my assumptions that others who spoke of his "total stupidity" knew the whole truth?*

The Power of Choice

We have so many choices we can make, including the choice to challenge—with kindness—our own divisive beliefs.

We are nearly always focused on something—whether we are conscious of this or not. You could say that we have two choices in life about how we focus: we can *actively* choose what we focus on, or we can *passively* allow the focus of our lives to be selected for us by the haphazardly accrued habits of our mind, by the otherizing forces in the media, and by the words and actions of others.

We can focus our own minds or have them focused for us: the former gives us power over our own lives; the latter creates dependency on whatever life serves up. When we choose thoughts that lead to less divisive, more elevated feelings, we tend to be happier.

CHAPTER 16

Transcending Divisiveness Makes You Happy

In the last two chapters, I mentioned some ways in which we have power over what we feel. We can change our state by changing our focus from stressful fight/flight emotions to the elevated and happier emotions of open heartedness.

We may have some resistance, however, to taking this step toward happiness. We may be habituated to living in stress, accustomed to the excitement of emergency mode, or addicted to the heat of anger. Of course, it's important to feel engaged, but this doesn't have to involve fight/flight emotions. Engagement without enragement is a much cooler arrangement.

I'm not saying that there's anything wrong with having emotional reactions to the events in our lives. It's natural to experience anger when things don't go according to plan. By fully accepting ourselves with all our feelings, including our anger, we are acting with kindness and respect toward ourselves. Full acceptance of our feelings is often helpful in letting them go—and this is useful, since a key to our well-being is our ability to move on from the emotional reverberations of the past.

When chased by a dog, a deer runs and bounds with terror-driven speed. Three minutes later, this same deer is calmly chewing grass and enjoying the pleasant sunshine. The deer does not hold on to angry judgments about the dog—probably because deer just don't *do* judgments. These creatures may sometimes be judged by us because they do not think as we do—but perhaps we can learn something from the deer's example of emotional dexterity.

Habits of Feeling

Emotional habits of fight/flight are so powerful that we can actually use political and other external situations to feed our addiction to stress, drama, and anger. Of course, we don't usually realize we're doing this. But if we have this common tendency and can recognize it, we have more power to choose differently. We are less likely to be sabotaged by our less-than-useful habits when we can see them coming.

Habits tend to last for a lifetime. This can be

a good thing or a bad thing, depending on the habit. The great thing (or terrible thing) about habits is that it is easier to follow a well-worn path than make a different one.

Putting this in neurological terms, the more you fire and wire electrical circuits in your brain through repetition of particular thoughts, feelings, or actions, the more you create electrical highways in which these patterns of thinking/feeling/action move with ease and speed. Changing from a habitual pattern to a new pattern takes extra effort initially, though once the path is beaten, it becomes easy.

Most personal change requires changing habits. As the Greek philosopher, and brilliant psychologist, Epictetus said around 100 CE:

> Whatever you would make habitual, practice it; and if you would not make a thing habitual, do not practice it, but accustom yourself to something else.

It's easy to get caught in a habit of stressful feelings, a habit of using the fight/flight response to get things done and to feel a certain kind of highly charged energy. The negative side of this you already know: the long-term secretion of stress hormones is associated with the many varieties of fearful and angry feelings, with judgmental and divisive thinking, with separation between self and other, and ultimately with poor health. The trap is that the more we practice this kind of reaction, the easier it is to repeat it. In fact, our responses can become so automatic that we stop thinking we have any choice.

But we *do* have a choice. We can, instead, practice a different set of emotions, the elevated emotions—like curiosity, wonder, compassion, calmness, warmth, contentment, inspiration, gratitude, care, love, humility, kindness, and respect. If this list seems like a lot to practice, the good thing is that all these qualities enhance each other. You only have to practice one for the others to grow.

Practicing Elevated Feelings

If you have read most of the chapters of this book, you will already have seen or practiced some of the elevated qualities: for example, *curiosity* in chapter 10; and *compassion* in the exercise on seeing from the other's point of view in chapter 13.

Both curiosity and compassion are powerful antidotes to the pain of otherizing and divisiveness.

- Curiosity reduces otherization because the curious person becomes interested in understanding the other's point of view. Understanding dissolves judgment and invites compassion.

- Compassion reduces otherization because compassionate people make a connection with human hearts, and this takes precedence over differences in belief.

In the scientific literature, what I'm calling elevated emotions are usually referred to as *character strengths* or *signature strengths*. Qualities like curiosity and compassion (or empathy) have been measured, and several statistical studies have shown a correlation of these character strengths with greater happiness and life satisfaction.

When we are curious, problems get reframed into the fun of puzzle-solving; when we are compassionate, we can feel the beautiful warmth of human connection, even at times of loss and hurt. Beyond these specific correlations, there is something else that is harder to define. All the elevated feelings are connecting rather than separating. When there is no *The Other* in our mind against whom we contract with fear or anger, the elevated emotions arise naturally and bring us to a feeling of connection and expansion. And this is a joy to experience.

How do we get to these elevated feelings that are correlated with peacefulness and happiness? Many people think they just don't have some of these qualities. But everyone has these qualities naturally. Curiosity, compassion, and kindness, for example, are foundational human instincts. To experience these qualities more often, all that is required is practice. The more we practice them, the easier it gets to feel their benefits and the more ingrained they become. And when they become ingrained, they begin to feel natural.

You can practice any of the elevated feelings. Google any of them and you will find all kinds of advice on how to practice them. However, there is one elevated feeling that is perhaps the easiest of all to develop, and that can be seen as a kind of shortcut to all the elevated feelings—gratitude.

Developing Gratitude

When as a kid, I was told to be grateful, I'd dutifully mumble, "Thank you." This did not lead to any elevated feelings.

But when as an adult, I had an open-hearted experience of gratitude, I realized that the feeling of gratitude had profound and exquisite dimensions, which were quite new to me. As I experienced the soft warmth of thankfulness, I felt bathed in an indefinable mixture of contentment, kindness, and love. It was such a beautiful feeling that I then felt deeply thankful for this gift of gratitude!

Gratitude dissolves the unpleasant experience of otherizing, resentment, and anger. It is actually impossible to feel gratitude and the anger/fear stress response at the same time.

This is because we have a choice of focusing on what we *don't* have (leading to resentment and otherizing) or focusing on what we *do* have (leading to gratitude). We cannot travel in both these opposite directions simultaneously because the brain can focus on only one thing at a time.

When we focus on what we don't have, or on what others have taken away from us, we tend to feel disappointed, sad, envious, jealous, or angry. And then we tend to blame others for what we think is their part in our deficit. In short, we hold a subliminal grudge that otherizes certain people or otherizes life in general. And we feel an unhappy aversion to anyone who we think is not giving us what we believe we are missing.

When we focus on what we do have, on the other hand, we feel a connection between ourselves and this perceived gift from life. There is a sense of oneness rather than otherization. Experiencing life's abundance, we feel happier. The best-selling author Sarah Ban Breathnach puts it this way:

> Both abundance and lack exist simultaneously in our lives, as parallel realities. It is always our conscious choice which secret garden we will tend.

The joy that emanates from the quality of gratitude has been stated by many spiritual writers and philosophers. In the early 1900s, author and philosopher G. K. Chesterton wrote,

> Thanks are the highest form of thought; gratitude is happiness doubled by wonder.

The writer David Steindl-Rast concurs:

> It is gratitude that makes us joyful.

More recently, such statements have been backed by statistical research. In one such study, subjects were asked to keep a diary once every day for two weeks. They were randomly assigned to one of three groups: group 1 wrote about matters they were grateful for; group 2 wrote about problems and hassles they encountered; while group 3 wrote descriptions of things that happened during the day. All participants were measured on a happiness scale before the experiment, and then again after the two weeks of writing. The happiness level in the gratitude group grew a full 25 percent, whereas the other two groups showed no increase on the happiness scale.

Many years ago I witnessed this effect in a twenty-seven-year-old man who consulted me because he felt suicidal. In contrast to his suicidal thoughts, he described several matters that had gone exceptionally well for him in the past week. Wondering about the reason for this discrepancy, I asked him if he kept a diary, and, when he replied in the affirmative, I asked him what kinds of things he wrote about. He replied: "I write about my problems, the things that went wrong in my childhood, all the things I feel bad about."

When I suggested that writing about what went wrong might be feeding his depressive thoughts, he disagreed: "But this is what I've been taught to write about. What I've understood from psychotherapy is that you have to get the bad stuff out in the open."

Rather than argue with him, I asked if he would be willing to try an experiment—for one week, write every day in his journal about everything that went well: his positive experiences, his moments of joy, his strengths.

When I saw him a week later, he smiled and said, "I can hardly believe it. I feel great. It's like I've been celebrating all the good things in my life. I've had no suicidal feelings. You know, I'm determined to continue what I started this week; I'm going to record the good things in my life..." Two years later, I happened to meet this man informally, and he told me that he had continued to focus on what went well for him, and that he'd had no recurrence of depressive or suicidal thoughts.

In January 2005, *Time* magazine ran a cover story on positive psychology, including the contribution of the psychologist Martin E. P. Seligman. Following this, thousands of people registered on a website, which had been created by Seligman and his colleagues at the Positive Psychology Center in the University of Pennsylvania. The website offered one free exercise, which involved writing down three things that went well during each day for one week. Of the thousands who did this exercise, fifty were severely depressed before the exercise (as measured on depression and happiness questionnaires). After the exercise, forty-seven of these fifty became significantly less depressed and much happier (as measured on the same depression and happiness questionnaires). This alleviation of suffering—and 47 out of 50 is an amazing result—apparently resulted from nothing more than writing down three things that went well at the end of each day.

In his book *Thanks! How the New Science of Gratitude Can Make You Happier*, the psychologist Robert A. Emmons shows that gratitude is also correlated with better health, higher performance, and improved relationships. Gratitude appears to be an antidote to resentment, bitterness, and greed—as well as to depression. And it is associated with joy, optimism, enthusiasm, and connectedness. All these associations are statistically verified.

In addition to being correlated with all these measurable positives, gratitude leads us very naturally to other elevated qualities. When we feel more *gratitude*, we experience the pleasure in a sense of personal abundance and the recognition that we have something to give; and that leads us to *kindness*. With gratitude, any grudge about how we think we have been treated unfairly in our lives is replaced with *contentment* about what we have received—therefore divisiveness dwindles. Without divisiveness, we are more compassionate. With *compassion*, we want to know what is going on for the other—we develop *curiosity*. And with curiosity comes greater *humility*, because we realize how much we do not know. Humility, in turn, leads back to greater *compassion*, for with more humility we can listen with fuller presence, without condescension or thinking we know what's wrong and how it should be fixed.

In such ways, gratitude leads us into a whole matrix of elevated feelings. All of them are antidotes to otherizing and all of them are pleasurable. These qualities tend to augment each other in upward spirals of joyful engagement. Gratitude is the magic carpet to the elevated feelings.

EXERCISE

Practice Gratitude

Here is the super-simple and time-honored way of developing more gratitude that I've already alluded to. Before going to bed, take five minutes each evening to write down at least three things that went well that day or that you are grateful for. The items you write down may seem to you to be small or large — it doesn't matter.

Here's what I wrote in my gratitude journal one evening just before turning the lights out for sleep:

Thank you

- For the feeling of peacefulness as I looked at the sky this morning.

- For getting through the pile of papers on my desk.

- For the woman in Shoprite saying "hello" so brightly.

- For that chocolate with hazelnut butter.

- For the beautiful tree outside my window.

Here are a few other examples that friends have shared with me: feeling the warmth of the sun, looking at the rain that enables all the plants to grow, being able to walk, electricity, completion of a mundane task, an experience of clarity, hot water to bathe in, a moment of kindness, a home in which to shelter, the beauty of a flower, a bowl of cereal, a smile of recognition.

Transcending Divisiveness Makes You Happy

By practicing elevated emotions, you are likely to become more effective in your dealings with other people. Those around you will pick up your state of mind and, through natural human empathy, will reflect your state back to you. The less *you* are driven by the stress hormones, the less *they* will be. The kinder you are, the kinder they will be.

There is no guarantee of this, of course, since other people make their own choices. But we always retain power over our own thinking and feeling—whatever may be happening in the country we live in and however aggravating may be our environment. When we work toward transcending divisiveness and reducing our own anger/fear responses—letting go of the contraction of battling *The Other*—then something magical happens: our hearts find the space to open to the pleasure of curiosity, compassion, gratitude, and kindness. And, though I don't know exactly why, each of these elevated qualities leads to yet more joy.

A few people have asked me about things they can do to help improve their general ability to deal with divisive or aversive energy. There are three that I've found especially effective: aerobic exercise, meditation, and taking action.

Aerobic Exercise

This is exercise of your cardiovascular and respiratory system. You know if you are doing it because you get at least a bit out of breath and your heart rate increases. I'm not going to go into the details of how to do this — there are hundreds of exercise regimes you can look up. You don't have to go overboard with this (just in case you were thinking you would) — twenty minutes of aerobic exercise three times a week is probably fine. If you are not already doing aerobic exercise and you are concerned whether you are medically OK to do it, please check with your doctor.

The reason aerobic exercise is so good for worry/fear or frustration/anger is that the exercise uses the hormones and nervous reactions that are created by the fight/flight physiological process. Aerobic exercise is also an excellent treatment for mild to moderate depression, as well as for anxiety, and it has no deleterious side-effects.

Aerobic exercise has, in addition, several beneficial side-effects—and they're not too shabby either. In addition to reducing depression and anxiety, moderate physical exercise has been proven to reduce our chances of developing dementia, diabetes, heart disease, high blood pressure, and hip fractures. Exercise increases mental capacity... oh, and also longevity. Of all the actions we can take that are statistically correlated with increased life-span, moderate aerobic exercise beats the lot of them—even more than reducing blood pressure or losing weight.

So, yeah, aerobic exercise is awesome.

One more thing—if you think of aerobic exercise as jogging and you hate jogging (I can relate to this one), don't worry. You do not need to jog. The thing is to find a way of exercising that you enjoy! It could be dancing, it could be walking or hiking, it could be a sport, or yoga, or swimming, or any fun exercise by yourself, with a partner, or with a group of friends.

Meditation

This is an exercise of the mind rather than the body—though its effects may also be physical (lowering blood pressure), emotional (transcending fear and anger), and spiritual (finding the peacefulness in which to connect to one's spiritual longing). Meditation involves deliberately shifting your focus from the world of outside concerns and worries to an inner world of peacefulness. I'm not going to go into the details of how to meditate, and, once again, there are many methods you can look up and many places where you can get training. Meditation requires an initial investment of ten to fifteen minutes of your time each day. If you make this investment, you may find, after a while, that you'd like to increase the time for daily meditation because of the benefits.

I mention in chapter 2 that repeated focus on anger and fear alters the structure of your brain — diminishing the size of parts of the pre-frontal cortex (associated with rationality), and increasing the size of the more primitive amygdala (associated with fight and flight). Meditation also changes the structure of your brain but in the opposite direction, increasing the size of parts of the prefrontal cortex and diminishing the size of the amygdala. Sara Lazar, neuroscientist at Harvard Medical School, found that these structural effects were visible on fMRI scans after only eight weeks of daily meditation.

In this book, I mention a few times the usefulness of focusing on commonality rather than differences. Meditation is one way of training this capacity.

Another theme in this book is the shifting from fight/flight divisive feelings to the elevated feelings of kindness, empathy, compassion, gratitude, joy, trust, and love. Meditation can take you there. Once your focus shifts from the outside world to an inner world of greater peacefulness, the elevated qualities arise naturally. They arise naturally because they are your birthright and because your mind is quiet and undistracted by stressful thoughts.

Taking Action

The more you practice the elevated qualities (in meditation, through the exercises in this book, or in practical situations with other people), the more natural they become to you and the easier it is for others to listen to you. In political situations, equanimity fuels your ability to fight smart without anger or rancor.

When you have concerns about what is happening in the world around you, no matter how divisive, there are always actions you can take. You can vote, you can phone, you can write, you can donate, you can demonstrate, you can offer your help, you can be kind. Your action does not have to be grand. Your contribution, whatever size, is an act of generosity that feeds both you and others. Service to a greater cause strengthens you.

Acknowledgments

I'm profoundly grateful to have been born in this beautiful world.

I thank my father, David, for his enquiring scientific mind. I thank my mother, Irena, for her courage and optimism.

For teaching on otherizing, I'm grateful to Mahatma Gandhi and Martin Luther King who were both exemplars of non-otherizing (even though they never used that word). Gandhi and King's examples have helped inform some of the practical suggestions I've given in this book. I also thank Marshall Rosenberg who, I think, translated Gandhi and King's non-violent approach into a step-by-step system through which people can find their natural compassion. I'm grateful to have been able to use some of his specific suggestions, which I know, from my own experience of trying them, can work.

For the teaching on the freedom of accepting complete responsibility for our feelings, I'm grateful to Epictetus, the wonderfully clear and practical ancient Greek psychologist.

For the understanding that freedom from anger comes from dropping expectations and demands—also mentioned by Epictetus—I'm grateful to some even more ancient teachings from Indian psychological/ philosophical texts. I had the good fortune to hear these teachings expounded by meditation masters who have lived and live these understandings. Thank you.

Thank you to Byron Katie for the Four Questions.

For the statistical studies on the relationship of character strengths and happiness, thank you to Martin Seligman, whose book *Flourish* was my introduction to this extensive research. And thank you to psychiatrist Elspeth McAdam for her dedication to teaching positive psychology before the term was coined. I learned the idea of looking back from a future vision from her technique of "back-lighting from the future."

To my editor Margaret Bendet, thank you for your invaluable advice on the content and the structure of this book. Thank you for lucidly pointing out better ways of writing a sentence or a paragraph, and for expertly balancing necessary corrections with listening for my intent in meaning.

Thank you to Caroline Wijetunge for your early reading of manuscripts and for your delicately presented nudges and suggestions.

Thank you to Randy Cale for your advice on building a platform and for our great discussions—and your ideas—that led to choosing the title of this book.

Thank you to Geoff Lindsey for the cover idea of having a stick-person thinking the title.

Thank you to Bea Murphy for helping me build my website and connecting it to this book, including finding systems for all the audio exercises in this book to be easily available for readers.

Thank you to Al Blanchard, Peter Hayes, Derek Chase, Laura Rogora, Claire James, John Martin, Lester Strong, David Haddad, Gita Haddad, Jennie Boyd Bull, David Katz, Marjorie Woollacott, Judith Levi, Pati Holland, Kenny Werner, Carol Sanford, Robert and Jane Alter, Monica Walsh, Jonathan Shimkin, and Irina Gillett for reading earlier drafts of the book, for offering me invaluable comments, and for going out of your way to be helpful.

Thank you to Tom and Carole Falkner for your ideas and encouragement.

Thank you to Stéphane Dehais for the cover, and for your design of the interior of this book. Thank you for your keen attention to detail, your patience and your artistry.

Thank you to Jacy Needles for your great support and encouragement. Thank you for your belief in this book, and thank you for the way you pass on this belief to others with so much enthusiasm.

Thank you to Arthur and Alexander, my sons, for your inspiring courage to take beneficial action in the world.

And thanks forever to Sanchi Kathryn Gillett, delightfully insightful partner in reading and in life, for all your comments on drafts of this book, and thank you for your encouragement to go back to writing after the publishing world had totally changed. And thank you for being my joint traveler to so many places and in so many wonderful ways.

NOTES

Preface

Page 2.

The *U.S. News & World Report* on divisiveness in the U.S. was published on February 21, 2019. The report quotes a poll conducted by the Public Religion Research Institute (PRRI), a nonprofit, nonpartisan research and education organization that conducts public opinion polls on a variety of different topics, specializing in the quantitative and qualitative study of political issues as they relate to religious values. According to this poll, 83 percent of Americans believe the country is divided by race and ethnicity. With regard to political division, 96 percent of Republicans and 91 percent of Democrats believe the country is very divided.

Chapter 1: Transcend Divisiveness

Page 11.

The particulars of Mylan's pricing for the EpiPen were garnered from several on-line sources, primarily Daniel Kozarich, Mylan's "Epipen Pricing Crossed Ethical Boundaries," *Fortune*, September 27, 2016, fortune.com/2016/09/27/mylan-epipen-heather-bresch/

Chapter 2: Emotion, Money, and Votes

Page 20.

With regard to the effect of anger (or fear) on the brain, see Daniel Goleman, *Social Intelligence: Why It Can Matter More Than IQ* (New York: Bantam, 2006), p. 225.

For evidence on the long-term structural changes in the brain caused by fear and anger, see the research article by Amy Arnsten, Carolyn M. Mazure, and Rajita Sinha, "Neural circuits responsible for conscious self-control are highly vulnerable to even mild stress. When they shut down, primal impulses go unchecked and mental paralysis sets in," Scientific American, April 2012, 306 (4), pp 48 – 53: available at the US National Library of Medicine, NIH: www.ncbi.nlm.nih.gov/pmc/articles/PMC4774859/

Page 23.

The study of the relationship between hostility and future coronary heart disease was carried out by John C. Barefoot, W. Grant Dahlstrom, and

Redford B. Williams, "Hostility, CHD Incidence, and Total Mortality: A 25-year Follow-up Study of 255 Physicians," *Psychosomatic Medicine*, vol. 45, issue 1 (1983), pp. 219 – 228.

The study of the relationship between hostility and future coronary heart disease in law students was carried out by John C. Barefoot, Kenneth A. Dodge, Bercedis L. Peterson, W. Grant Dahlstrom, and Redford B. Williams, "The Cook-Medley Hostility Scale: Item Content and Ability to Predict Survival," *Psychosomatic Medicine*, vol. 51, issue 1 (1989), pp. 46 – 57.

In 2009, Y. Chida and A. Steptoe from the University of London did a meta-analytic review of 39 studies on this subject in which they concluded, "The current review suggests that anger and hostility are associated with CHD [coronary heart disease] outcomes both in healthy and CHD populations." From "The association of anger and hostility with future coronary heart disease: a meta-analytic review of prospective evidence," *Journal of the American College of Cardiology* 2009 March 17, vol. 53, no. 11, pp. 936 – 46; doi: 10.1016/j.jacc.2008.11.044

Chapter 3: How Divisive Emotions Can Save or Ruin Your Life

Page 33.

Brain changes during fight and flight reactions are well documented. In summary, the transfer of neuronal impulses across synapses in the prefrontal cortex is diminished or shut down during stress. At the same time the dominance of the evolutionarily older parts of the brain—such as the hypothalamus—is augmented. The result is a greater focus on instant emotion and action, as opposed to thinking or planning. The primary benefit of this switch of brain energy is the speed of response. For example, someone may be able to jump out of the way of an oncoming vehicle before having a single thought. Thinking is a slower process. The negative side is that prolonged stress has a long-term effect on the prefrontal cortex, including damage to neural structures. See (also referred to in the notes from chapter 2) Amy Arnsten, Carolyn M. Mazure, and Rajita Sinha, "Neural circuits responsible for conscious self-control are highly vulnerable to even mild stress. When they shut down, primal impulses go unchecked and mental paralysis sets in," Scientific American, April 2012, 306 (4), pp 48 – 53: available at the US National Library of Medicine, NIH: **www.ncbi.nlm.nih.gov/pmc/articles/PMC4774859/**

Chapter 4: The Tyrannosaurus in the Room

Page 37.

In regard to the use of the word *ego*, the English word *egoity* was used in 1651, and referred to "that which forms the essence of the individual"—*Oxford English Dictionary*. The English words, *egoism, egoist, egotism, egotistical,* and *ego* followed. In the early 20ᵗʰ century, Freud put forward a model of the psyche which we now know as *id, ego,* and *super-ego*. But Freud did not actually use these terms himself, since he wrote in German. Freud's German word *"das Ich"* *("the I")* got translated by his English translator—unfortunately, and confusingly—into "ego." By *"das Ich"* Freud was referring largely to the reasoning power of the self, quite different from what was understood by *ego*, which had existed in the English language for more than a century before Freud's hypothesized model. Since Freud's time, some Western psychologists have gone back to using *ego* in its original sense (pride in individual difference), but this has created confusion for some others. Many psychologists avoid using the word *ego* because of this confusion. The psychoanalyst, Karen Horney, who wrote *Neurosis and Human Growth: The Struggle Towards Self-Realization* (Oxfordshire, U.K.: Routledge, 1951*)*, described at length what could, according to the English dictionary, be called *ego*, but used the word *pride* instead. Meanwhile the word *ego* has retained its original meaning in broad public usage.

Page 38.

"Self-esteem is how we feel about ourselves, while the ego is how we compare ourselves to others." This succinct comparison is what the dance-teacher Eveline Carle tells her pupils at the Cape Cod Dance Center. The quote comes from her book: Eveline Carle, *Dancing Feat*, (Lancaster, PA: Willow Moon Publishing, 2018) p. 131.

Page 39.

"Your body contains, for example, more electrons than there are grains of sand on this earth!" For a simple explanation of the estimated number of electrons in the human body, see JLab Science Education, at **education.jlab.org/qa/mathatom_04.html**. The figure is generally estimated as around 2×10^{28} (2 followed by 28 zeros). To get the number of grains of sand on earth, scientists in Hawaii, possibly inspired by their local beaches, counted the number of grains of sand in a teaspoon and then calculated the number of teaspoons of sand in all the deserts and beaches in the world. The result? Only about 7.5×10^{18} grains of sand—that means, if these calculations are reasonably accurate, that a human body has more than a billion electrons for every grain of sand on earth.

For the number of cells in the human body, see **www.ncbi.nlm.nih. gov/pubmed/23829164**. To estimate how long it would take to count 37 trillion, I timed how many numbers I could count in a minute (180) and multiplied this by 60 (minutes in an hour), then by 24, by 365, and by 80 (assuming a lifetime of 80 years). This gives a figure of 7.57 billion numbers counted in an 80-year lifetime without stopping to sleep, eat, talk, etc. Dividing 37 trillion by 7.57 billion gives a figure of 4,887 lifetimes.

Chapter 5: Protect Yourself from Divisive Influences in the Media

Page 58.

The quote from the press critic A. J. Liebling is from his essay "The Wayward Press: Do You Belong in Journalism," which was printed in May 16, 1960, in *The New Yorker*, pg. 109: **www.newyorker.com/magazine/1960/05/14/do-you-belong-in-journalism**

Page 59.

Rupert Murdoch's orders to the editors of the *Sun* in March 1997, and the effect of this on votes for the Labour Party, were discussed in Aaron Reeves, Martin McKee, and David Stuckler, "It's the Sun Wot Won It: Evidence of media influence on political attitudes and voting from a UK quasi-natural experiment," *Social Science Research, Vol. 56, March 2016, pp. 44 – 57,* **dx.doi.org/10.1016/j.ssresearch.2015.11.002**

Page 61.

For the MarketWatch article on the Media Bias Chart, see Shawn Langlois, *MarketWatch*, published April 21, 2018, "How biased is your news source? You probably won't agree with this chart": **www.marketwatch. com/story/how-biased-is-your-news-source-you-probably-wont-agree-with-this-chart-2018-02-28**

Chapter 6: Protect Yourself from Divisive Influences in Party Politics

Page 67.

Sybil Carrere and John Gottman, "Predicting Divorce Among Newlyweds from the First Three Minutes of a Marital Conflict Discussion," *Family Process* 38, no.3 (1999): 293 – 301. See also the book by J. M. Gottman, et al, *The Mathematics of Marriage: Dynamic Nonlinear Models* (Cambridge, MA: MIT Press, 2005).

Page 71.

Figures for the history of popular support for gay marriage in the U.S. can be found in the article "Attitudes on Same Sex Marriage," PEW Research Center: Religion and Public Life fact sheet, May 14, 2019: **www.pewforum.org/fact-sheet/changing-attitudes-on-gay-marriage/** The graph in this article shows the percentage of people who supported gay marriage (which had been gradually increasing over many years) surpassed the percentage of people who opposed gay marriage in 2011, one year before the Democratic Party began to support gay marriage publicly.

In 1972, a Gallup poll showed that 68 percent of Republicans and 59 percent of Democrats agreed that "the decision to have an abortion should be made solely by a woman and her physician." Evangelical Christians took an anti-abortion stance after Roe vs. Wade in 1973, contending that easily accessible abortion encouraged sexual promiscuity in women. Evangelical Christians became an important source of votes for the Republican party, and, starting with Nixon, the Republican party has increasingly supported an anti-abortion stance. See the column by Joshua Tate, "How Did Evangelicals and Republicans Come to Want to Ban Abortion," ARCdigital, May 1, 2019, **arcdigital.media/how-did-evangelicals-and-republicans-come-to-oppose-abortion-dcd4ac56c333**

Page 74.

The hypnosis study on pre-birth experiences and the subject of the time of ensoulment is described in Helen Wambach, *Life Before Life* (New York: Bantam, 1979) p. 98 – 121.

Page 77.

In January 21, 2010, the US Supreme Court overruled Austin v. Michigan Chamber of Commerce (1990), which had allowed different restrictions on speech-related spending based on corporate identity, as well as a portion of McConnell v. FEC (2003) that had restricted corporate spending on electioneering communications. This ruling effectively allowed corporations to fund election campaign advertisements.

Chapter 7: The Pleasure of Dropping Anger, and How to Do It

Page 84.

The Greek philosopher Epictetus lived c 55 – 135 CE. Epictetus wrote nothing that has survived. Fortunately, a student, Arrian, took notes on

Epictetus's teachings and these have survived for nearly two millennia. The line quoted in the text is from *Enchiridion* 20, translated by P. E. Matheson, The Discourses and Manual, two vols. (Oxford, U.K., Clarendon Press, 1916) www.letsreadgreek.com/epictetus/mattheson.htm#c20

In *Enchiridion* 5, Epictetus says: "Events don't disturb us; it's the attitudes we take toward events that disturb us." This translation is by Stephen Walton, *The Manual or How to Control Everything You Can: A Modern Rendering of the Enchiridion by Epictetus*, 1997, www.ideonautics.net/manual2.htm.

Page 88.

This quote from Martin Luther King Jr. is taken from "Beyond Vietnam: A Time to Break Silence," a speech he gave at a meeting of clergy and laity at Riverside Church in New York City on April 4, 1967.

Page 91.

The exercise is derived from three main sources. The first is Epictetus from nearly 2,000 years ago (see the first note on this chapter). The second is the even more ancient Indian psychological/philosophical systems (as exemplified, for instance, in the Bhagavad Gita), which show how anger is caused by thwarted desire—the converse being that dropping the desire (expectation) for a particular result causes anger to abate. The third is Marshall Rosenberg's much more recent presentation of Nonviolent Communication. See Marshall B. Rosenberg, Nonviolent Communication: A Language of Life (Encinitas, CA: PuddleDancer Press, 1999).

Chapter 8: Handle Others' Anger Brilliantly

Page 97.

The sardonic quote of President Kennedy about Bull Connor helping the civil rights movement is from the book by Flip Schulke and Penelope Ortner McPhee, *King Remembered* (New York: Pocket Books, 1986) p. 132.

Page 98.

After the passage of the Civil Rights Act (1964) and the Voting Rights Act (1965), African Americans entered the political arena. Between 1963 and 1984, the number of African American elected officials in the South grew 7000 percent (from a total of 50 to 3,498). From *King Remembered*, p. 266.

Page 101.

The homicide statistics are from the U.S. Census Bureau, Statistical Abstract of the United States: 2007, table 299. This table gives the rates for homicide, based on different motivations, between the years 1990 and 2004.

Page 104.

Marshall Rosenberg's presentation of Nonviolent Communication in Palestine, when he was called a murderer, is described in more detail in his book, *Nonviolent Communication: A Language of Life*, cited in the last note for chapter 7. The story is on pp. 13 – 14.

Page 106.

For a full description of how to link feelings with needs/wishes, see Rosenberg's excellent book, *Nonviolent Communication*.

Chapter 9: Decide What Is within Your Own Power

Page 111.

Clarifying that which is and is not in our power to accomplish was recommended by the ancient Greek philosopher Epictetus, whose question to his students was this: "Is it concerned with what is in our power or with what is not in our power?" This is from *Enchiridion 1*, translated by P. E. Matheson. See P.E. Matheson (translator), *Epictetus: Discourses and Manual* (Oxford, UK, Clarendon Press, 1916). In recent years, many influential self-help and leadership books have emphasized this point. Stephen Covey, in *The Seven Habits of Highly Effective People* (New York: Simon and Schuster, 1989), refers to differentiating between our "circle of concern" and our smaller "circle of influence," and recommends focusing on the latter.

The quotation on expectations attributed to Benjamin Franklin is also attributed to the poet Alexander Pope and to the essayist Jonathan Swift. It is possible that Franklin was quoting one of these other two men, or he may have come up with this line independently. The idea of unfulfilled expectation creating disappointment—or unfulfilled desires creating anger—exists in the recorded teachings of Epictetus and, predating Epictetus, in the *Bhagavad Gita* and other ancient Indian texts.

Chapter 10: The Liberating Power of Curiosity

Page 115.

Albert Einstein's comment on never losing a holy curiosity was made to William Miller, as quoted in LIFE magazine, Vol 38, No 18, May 2, 1955, p. 64.

Page 118.

In 2018, the average time spent watching video in the U.S. was just under six hours per day according to Sarah Parez, "U.S. Adults now spend nearly 6 hours per day watching video," *TechCrunch*, July 31, 2018, techcrunch.com/2018/07/31/u-s-adults-now-spend-nearly-6-hours-per-day-watching-video/

If you would like to measure your level of curiosity, you can do so on the VIA Strengths Survey on www.authentichappiness.org.

Page 120.

The book on history from an Islamic point of view is by Tamim Ansary, *Destiny Disrupted: A History of the World Through Islamic Eyes*, (Philadelphia, PA: PublicAffairs, 2009).

Two articles are cited on CIA involvement. Saeed Kamali Dehghan and Richard Norton-Taylor, "CIA Admits Role in Iranian Coup," *Guardian*, August 19, 2013: www.theguardian.com/world/2013/aug/19/cia-admits-role-1953-iranian-coup. Bethany Allen-Ebrahimian, "Report: 64 Years Later, CIA Finally Releases Details of Iranian Coup," *Guardian*, June 20, 2017: foreignpolicy.com/2017/06/20/64-years-later-cia-finally-releases-details-of-iranian-coup-iran-tehran-oil/

Page 125.

With regard to sociological research on reasons why people voted one way or another in the U.S. elections in 2016, see the following non-politically aligned survey: Robert Griffin and Ruy Teixeira, "The Story of Trump's Appeal," *Voter Study Group*, June 2017, www.voterstudygroup.org/publication/story-of-trumps-appeal

According to this survey, 52 percent of those who voted for Trump said their personal finances had gotten worse since 2012, while only 26 percent of Clinton voters thought the same. Of Trump voters, 59 percent believed the economy was worse since 2012 compared to just over a quarter of this figure (15 percent) of Clinton voters.

With regard to working-class anger with the Democratic Party in the U.S., in January 2018, Thomas Piketty, the French political economist, wrote a detailed analysis—with an enormous amount of data and 106 pages of graphs and charts—on the results of post-election surveys in Britain, the United States, and France between 1948 and 2017. The paper is posted by the World Inequality Lab. What Piketty found is that the kind of voter who historically supported liberal-democratic parties—the Left—tended to be poorer and less educated. In the last two decades, however, the liberal-democratic parties have become increasingly centrist, coming up with policies that appeal to the rich elites—who are also donors. At the same time, wages for the poor have stagnated while profits for the rich have increased enormously. The lower-echelon wage earners saw that they were no longer supported by the very politicians they were voting into office. Looking for something new, these voters were drawn to populist candidates—candidates who promised a change. The change these candidates offered was to re-identify the problem. Where the liberal-democratic parties had always pointed to the rich—society's 1 percent—as the problem, now the populists were saying that the problem was minorities and immigrants. Piketty's article is entitled: "Brahmin Left vs. Merchant Right: Rising Inequality & the Changing Structure of Political Conflict." Some of the content is summarized by Keith A. Spencer, *Salon*, June 2, 2019, www.salon.com/2019/06/02/

Chapter 11: The Relief of Seeing the Bigger Picture

Page 131.

The classification of the ancient Chinese view of moral ascent is from Abraham Kaplan, *The New World of Philosophy* (New York: Random House Vintage Books, 1961) pp. 295 – 96.

Page 133.

Here, summarized from the Kaplan book, are the higher two levels of the ancient Chinese classification of moral attainment:

> ### Level 4—The morality of oneness.
> At this level, the person is at one with herself. She is "at peace with her own intrinsic nature." She has genuineness, integrity, and natural goodness. Her compassion extends naturally to all humanity and to the earth on which we live.

> ### Level 5—The morality of enlightenment
> At this highest level of spiritual attainment, the enlightened being identifies with that which transcends all division—whether it is called God, the Self, the essence of the universe, or any other of the many names it has been given. Here, all expectations are transcended. The enlightened one radiates goodness and gives what is most needed, whether others understand this or not.

These fourth and fifth levels involve the recognition of oneness in all people and in everything. From the scientific perspective, the unity that underlies all things is the energetic substratum from which all matter is created. From the spiritual perspective, the unity that underlies everything is the fundamental Reality. Those who live in the experience of this state of unity consciousness describe a world of unconditional love and supreme bliss in which gratitude, compassion, and kindness shine effortlessly, like gems in the light of the gaze of the highest intelligence.

Page 136.

With regard to wealth inequality in the U.S., see Avery Anapol, "Study: Wealthiest 1 percent owns 40 percent of country's wealth," *The Hill*, December 6, 2017, **thehill.com/news-by-subject/finance-economy/363536-study-wealthiest-1-percent-own-40-percent-of-countrys-wealth**

The Hitler, Stalin, and Mao death toll of 70 million is composed of 10 million by Hitler, 20 million by Stalin, and 40 million by Mao. These numbers are from Matthew White's "The 30 Worst Atrocities of the 20th Century," *The Historical Atlas of the 20th Century*, **users.erols.com/mwhite28/atrox.htm**. To obtain a figure for deaths by atrocity, White used a large array of published sources and took the median figure as a reasonably conservative estimate.

Page 141.

Deregulation of the banks, beginning in the Reagan years and continued by both Republican and Democratic presidents, created the increasing riskiness in the banking industry that resulted in the 2008 financial debacle. The self-interested influence of the banking industry was expanded by the fact that former bankers were given leadership positions in the U.S. Treasury. Here are three examples: 1) Lewis Sachs, a member of the board of directors of Bear Stearns, became assistant secretary of the Treasury for Financial Markets between 1999 and 2001. Later, Sachs returned to the finance sector as the CEO of Cornerstone Asset Management. 2) Robert Rubin, co-chairman of Goldman Sachs, became treasury secretary under President Clinton. Later he returned to banking as a board director of Citigroup. 3) Henry Paulson, CEO of Goldman Sachs, became treasury secretary under President George Bush.

Regarding Rupert Murdoch's orders to the editors of the *Sun* in March 1997, see the second note for chapter 5.

Page 144.

The Time Travel exercise contains a technique called *back-lighting from the future*, which was developed by Dr. Elspeth McAdam and Dr. Peter Lang.

I learned of this technique from Dr. McAdam in an interview I had with her on March 17, 2012. If we look ahead at the steps we need to take to create success in the future (i.e. looking into the future from the present), obstacles tend to loom large because, from our present position, we don't know if we can get through them. But if we look back from a future in which the goal is already attained, then we "know" each step can be accomplished.

McAdam and Lang were also influenced by the philosopher, John Dewey, who wrote of how the present can be more influenced by the future that by the past. This seems a surprising statement at first because we are so versed in the paradigm of seeing cause from the past creating effect in the present. In simple mechanical systems this paradigm works well: the present height the ball bounces is due to the past velocity with which it hit the ground. But with the mind, it is different. The mind is so complex, so versatile, so blessed with choice, that it is not forced to move in any particular direction by past events. However, the mind can create a future vision from which it can energize its choices and decisions for action. The past is often seen as limiting or negative. The future vision draws like a magnet and can be as expansive and positive as we would like it to be. The past seems immutable, as if denying our free will and responsibility. The future, by contrast, is ours to create. We each have the choice to create our present from pieces we select from the past, or from the vision of the future we aspire to. Does past or future create the present for the human mind and feelings? It's up to us.

Chapter 12: Beyond All Prejudice

Page 149.

With regard to the 99.99 percent genetic identity between members of different races, the figure comes initially from a consensus of scientific opinion that human beings from all over the world are 99.9 percent genetically identical. See an abstract by F.S. Collins and M.K. Mansoura, "The Human Genome Project: Revealing the shared inheritance of all humankind," *PubMed*, the NCBI (National Center for Biotechnology Information) website: **www.ncbi.nlm.nih.gov/pubmed/11148583/**. Of the 0.1% genetic variation between human beings, there is some debate about what percentage of this tiny percentage creates racial differences, but there is consensus that the racial marker percentage (i.e., genes that are expressed as skin color, characteristic facial features, etc.) is a very small fraction of the 0.1 percent overall genetic variation. If this fraction is as much as 10%, that would give a figure of 0.01 percent genetic differences between races.

Page 150.

The African origin of human beings is summarized by Elizabeth Kolbert in "There's No Scientific Basis for Race—It's a Made-Up Label," *National Geographic*, April 2018: www.nationalgeographic.com/magazine/2018/04/race-genetics-science-africa/

Page 154.

Malcolm Gladwell discussed his personal experience of the IAT in his book *Blink: The Power of Thinking Without Thinking* (New York: Little, Brown, 2005) pp. 77 – 86.

Page 155.

That an American black man is thirteen times more likely than a white man to go to jail for an identical drug-related crime is discussed by Gladwell in Blink, p. 275. The figures Gladwell reports come from the nonprofit group Human Rights Watch.

Page 159.

Overcoming prejudice through taking time to be with the people one is prejudiced against was explained by Gordon Allport in his 1954 book, *The Nature of Prejudice*. This became known as Allport's "contact hypothesis" (i.e., contact diminishes prejudice). See Gordon Allport, *The Nature of Prejudice*, Oxford, England: Addison-Wesley, 1954. Since this book's publication, Allport's point has been backed up repeatedly by researchers who have measured the significant reductions in prejudice that follow spending time with the *other* person or group. You can see this summarized in John Dovidio, Peter Glick, Laurie Rudman, *On the Nature of Prejudice: Fifty Years After Allport*, (Hoboken, NJ: Wiley, 2005).

The research on the amygdala lighting up when we see members of groups that we don't consider our own comes from Rudolfo Mendoza-Denton, Jason Marsh, and Jeremy Adam Smith (editors), *Are We Born Racist? New Insights from Neuroscience and Positive Psychology* (Boston, MA: Beacon, 2010).

Chapter 13: Reconnecting with Family and Friends

Page 175.

This exercise to end lingering anger after a disagreement is based on the timeless advice of putting yourself in someone else's shoes. This particular iteration of the technique is adapted from Neuro-Linguistic

Programming (NLP), a therapeutic methodology developed by Richard Bandler and John Grinder in the 1970s. Bandler and Grinder's methods were, in turn, derived from their careful study of three exceptional therapists: Milton Erickson, Virginia Satir, and Fritz Perls. The technique also has deeper roots in philosophical and religious texts which extol the value of detachment and compassion.

Chapter 14: The Amazing Richness of Personal Choice

Page 181.

For an informative article on how Facebook and other social media organizations make money through enhancing public fear and outrage, see Tobias Rose-Stockwell, "This is how your fear and outrage are being sold for a profit," *Quartz*, July 2017, qz.com/1039910/how-facebooks-news-feed-algorithm-sells-our-fear-and-outrage-for-profit/

Page 184.

With regard to political situations changing quite quickly, an interview with Salman Rushdie in which he makes similar points is "Salman Rushdie On His New Novel, A Reality-Bending Journey Through Trump's America," on *WGBH News*, September 16, 2019, www.wgbh.org/news/arts/2019/09/16/salman-rushdie-on-his-new-novel-a-reality-bending-journey-through-trumps-america/

Chapter 15: Choose Your Thoughts, Choose Your Feelings

Page 188.

With regard to *mental cliffs*, this idea comes from a sonnet by Gerard Manley Hopkins:

> O the mind, mind has mountains; cliffs of fall
> Frightful, sheer, no-man-fathomed..."

The lines are from Hopkins, *Poems and Prose* (London: Penguin Classics, 1985) p. 61.

Page 190.

The number of thoughts the mind thinks each day has been variously estimated as between 10,000 and 70,000. However, there are no references that I could find for these figures—numbers that tend to get copied from book to book. Also, what constitutes a single thought remains undefined. Suffice to say that we think a very large number of thoughts each day.

Page 193.

These four questions are the subject of Byron Katie's book *Loving What Is: Four Questions That Can Change Your Life*, (New York: Random House, 2002).

Page 195.

Ivanka Trump's use of private emails for government business is reported by Matthew Daly, "House Dems back subpoenas for Ivanka, Jared private emails," *Associated Press News*, July 25, 2019, www.apnews.com/af2ec002e0f945909dd52b68410748db

A summary of the facts regarding Hilary Clinton's official emails on her private server are listed by Eugene Kiely, "A Guide to Clinton's Emails," *FactCheck*, October 28, 2016, www.factcheck.org/2016/07/a-guide-to-clintons-emails/

Page 196.

mediaQuant's estimate of over $5 billion in free media reporting on Donald Trump, during his election campaign, was reported by Ginger Gibson and Grant Smith, "At under $5 each, Trump's votes came cheap," *Reuters*, November 9, 2016, www.reuters.com/article/us-usa-election-spending/at-under-5-each-trumps-votes-came-cheap-idUSKBN1341JR

Chapter 16: Transcending Divisiveness Makes You Happy

Page 203.

Regarding the popular quote on habits by Epictetus, this is from *Discourses*, book 2, chapter 18.

Page 205.

Regarding measurement of character strengths, in 2004, the psychologists Christopher Peterson and Martin Seligman developed a measurement tool called the "VIA Strengths Survey." This survey measures twenty-four character strengths that are recognized across various cultures. These character strengths include, though are broader than, what I am calling "the elevated feelings." You can take their survey at **www.authentichappiness.sas.upenn.edu/questionnaires/survey-character-strengths**

Many studies link character strengths with happiness. In one study by Park et al, hope, zest, gratitude, curiosity, and love, were found to be the character strengths most highly correlated with life satisfaction. These results came from a sample of 3,907 individuals across different countries and cultures. N. Park, C. Peterson, M. P. Seligman, "Strengths of Character and Well-Being," *Journal of Social and Clinical Psychology,* 2004, no. 23, pp. 603–19.

Also see A. M. Wood, P. A. Linley, J. Maltby, T. B. Kashdan, and R. Hurling, "Personality and Individual Differences," *Journal of Social and Clinical Psychology,* 2011, no. 50, pp. 15–19. Using personal and psychological strengths leads to increases in well-being over time: a longitudinal study and the development of the strengths use questionnaire.

That qualities like curiosity, compassion, and kindness are intrinsic instincts comes from multiple studies on mammals, including human beings. One such study on toddlers, all aged less than two years, showed that these young children experienced significantly more pleasure from giving than they did from receiving. See Lara B. Aknin, J. Kiley Hamlin, and Elizabeth W. Dunn, "Giving Leads to Happiness in Young Children," *PLOS ONE,* 2012; 7(6): e39211, published online 2012 June 14: **www.researchgate.net/publication/227712713_Giving_Leads_to_ Happiness_in_Young_Children**

Page 207.

Sarah Ben Breathnach is the author of *Simple Abundance: A Daybook of Comfort and Joy* (New York: Warner Books, 1995). Her book has sold 7 million copies.

Page 208.

G. K. Chesterton, British philosopher and detective story writer, 1874 – 1936, was a champion of the wonder of gratitude. The full passage from which this quote came is, "I would maintain that thanks are the highest form of thought, and that gratitude is happiness doubled by wonder." Chesterton also wrote: "When it comes to life, the critical thing is whether you take things for granted or take them with gratitude."

The experiment that showed that writing on gratitude increased happiness and life satisfaction comes from R. Emmons and M. McCullough, "Counting blessings versus burdens: An experimental investigation of gratitude and subjective well-being in daily life," *Journal of Personality and Social Psychology,* 2003, vol. 84, no. 2, 377 – 89. This was also quoted by Martin Seligman in his book *Flourish: A Visionary New Understanding of Happiness and Well-Being* (New York: Free Press, 2011) p. 74.

Page 210.

The story about the *Time* magazine article on positive psychology and the later study that showed an inverse correlation of gratitude and depression comes from Martin Seligman, *Flourish*, (New York: Simon and Schuster, 2011), p. 43.

Robert A. Emmons, *Thanks! How the New Science of Gratitude Can Make You Happier* (New York: Houghton Mifflin Harcourt, 2007). Emmons is a psychologist who has specialized in the study of gratitude.

Afterword

Page 216.

For the evidence on structural changes in the brain following meditation, see S. W. Lazar et al., "Meditation Experience Is Associated with Increased Cortical Thickness," *Neuroreport* 16, no. 17 (2005): 1893-97. This subject is discussed in the neuroscientist Marjorie Woollacott's book: Marjorie Woollacott, *Infinite Awareness*, (New York, Rowan and Littlefield, 2015), pp. 18-20.

About the Author

Physician, psychiatrist, keynote speaker, and author Richard Gillett received his medical degree from Cambridge University, England, and is a member of the Royal College of Psychiatrists. His work is based on a lifelong personal and professional quest—what does it take for a human being to lead the best possible life, even when circumstances are rough? This quest took him all over the world—he has lived on four continents—and led him to settle in New York State in 1991, where he was granted residency as a "professional of extraordinary ability" before he naturalized as a U.S. citizen. He currently lives in New York with his wife, not far from their two sons and their families.

In his years of research in various countries and cultures, Richard Gillett came to the understanding that much of our suffering is created by a common habit—divisiveness—a mindset that is relatively easy for us to change once we see how we're doing it.

DoctorGillett.com

Made in the USA
Middletown, DE
15 July 2020

12894148R00139